The soloing section of the book starts with exercises to help you develop your right-hand technique. Next, you'll learn the common arpeggios that form the basis for improvising in the style. Each of the following chapters is devoted to a specific technique. You'll also learn some go-to intros and outros that will work on just about any tune. The last chapter of the book is comprised of ten solo examples that incorporate all the previously learned techniques with analysis. In addition, there are backing tracks for you to practice soloing over. I've used traditional chord diagrams (read vertically), as well as arpeggio shape diagrams that are read horizontally.

In a rather major departure from other guitar methods, I didn't include any scales in this book. This may seem like blasphemy, so let me explain: in all my years of teaching guitar, I noticed that many of my students knew the basic scales but were incapable of playing even the simplest arpeggio. To them, they seemed to be two distinct entities when, in fact, they are part of the same thing. I would argue that the arpeggio is more important. A scale gives you a list of notes you can play over a chord, but that's not enough information. The arpeggio is much more precise; it teaches you which notes you can resolve to and which notes add color, or tension. Some scales will be referenced throughout the book, but arpeggios will be the foundation on which we build our vocabulary.

In addition to the exercises, history, and backing tracks provided, many of these concepts are demonstrated in video lessons, which are all accessible by going to *www.halleonard.com/mylibrary* and inputting the code found on page 1. Now, let's jump in!

CHAPTER 1

HISTORY OF GYPSY JAZZ GUITAR

Dave Rubin

The Romani People

The Romani people are the predecessors of Gypsies, originating in northern India around the 10th century and possibly forced out by expanding Islam or famine. Their story is frequently one of persecution and slavery, and lack of a written language and an origin story makes pinpointing specifics difficult. However, genetic evidence connects the Romani people to the descendants of groups which emigrated from South Asia towards Central Asia during the medieval period. By the 14th century, they had reached the Balkans and Bohemia. Traveling through Europe in the 15th century were the two main and separate tribes: the Manouche Roma, or *Sinti*, with ties in France, Germany, Austria, and Italy, by way of the Middle East, and the Gitane Roma through Spain. The 16th century found Romanies in Russia, Denmark, Scotland, and Sweden. The word "Roma" was the Romani word for "people." Due to their dark complexion, Europeans erroneously believed them to be from Egypt, and corrupted "Egyptian" into "Gypsy," the term first appearing in English in the early 15th century. Adding to the inherent diversity, the French language distinguishes between Manouches as French-speaking, Romanies who speak Italian, Gitanes who speak Spanish, and the Central European Bohémiens who speak a German dialect.

Music played an extremely important part in the lives of the historically nomadic Romani people, dating back to the playing of instruments such as the lute in the 1400s in Hungary and Italy. Wherever they roamed, they were recognized as musicians while exhibiting Indian, Byzantine, Greek, Persian, Arabic, Turkish, Slavic, Romanian, German, Dutch, French, Jewish, and Spanish influences. Indeed, flamenco music springs to a degree from the Romani Gitano music and culture of Andalusia. In Eastern Europe, however, another strain of Romani music developed to be played outside the community for dances and other celebrations, showing, among other roots, those of Hungary, Russia, and Romania. Eventually, this Romani music gained favor in Western Europe from the 1850s on with Romani orchestras preceding the evolution to Gypsy jazz. Their sophisticated music would enjoy popularity into the 20th century, particularly in France, peaking in the 1920s.

Django

"Out of the ten best guitar players in the world, Reinhardt was five of them."

–Rex Stewart, cornetist with the Duke Ellington band.

The legendary Manouche Gypsy Jean "Django" Reinhardt (1910–1953) was born away from Paris in Liberchies, Belgium on January 23, 1910. Though it may be the diminutive of Jean, "Django" is generally believed to be a Gypsy name meaning, "I awake." If so, it could not have been more prescient. Such began the legend of arguably the greatest jazz guitarist ever.

The Beginning: 1922–1928

Django exhibited a keen interest in music as a child and begged his mother for a guitar. A photo from 1923 shows him holding a six-string banjo-guitar. He quickly advanced on his own and, at around 13, played with an accordionist in a notorious type of dance hall known as a *bal-musette*. Soon, he was accompanying others, sitting in with his developing style and knowledge of American songs. In 1928, an English bandleader made a special trip to Paris to hear Django improvise jazz and made him an offer to join his orchestra. An agreement was reached on October 25, 1928 to meet the next night for the signing of a contract.

The Fire and Birth of a Legend

In the wee small hours of October 26, 1928, 18-year-old Django returned to his horse-drawn caravan in the Gypsy "zone" after his Paris gig. His wife awoke and reached for a match to light a candle. It fell on a pile of highly flammable artificial flowers, bursting into flames and engulfing the caravan in a matter of minutes. Django was burned before he could escape, covered in flames which his neighbors smothered on the ground. His left hand and right leg were severely injured. A hospital surgeon wanted to amputate his leg, but Django wisely resisted, and his friends spirited him away to a nursing home where he spent 18 grueling months recuperating. In an effort to lift his spirits, a doctor compassionately requested a guitar be brought to his bedside. Over time and through sheer willpower, Django devised a way to play again despite having

HAL LEONARD GYPSY JAZZ GUITAR METHOD

BY JEFF MAGIDSON & DAVE RUBIN

CONTENTS

To access video and audio visit:
www.halleonard.com/mylibrary

Enter Code
3907-7597-7171-2578

ISBN 978-1-5400-2147-2

Visit Hal Leonard Online at
www.halleonard.com

World headquarters, contact:
Hal Leonard
7777 West Bluemound Road
Milwaukee, WI 53213
Email: info@halleonard.com

In Europe, contact:
Hal Leonard Europe Limited
42 Wigmore Street
Marylebone, London, W1U 2RY
Email: info@halleonardeurope.com

In Australia, contact:
Hal Leonard Australia Pty. Ltd.
4 Lentara Court
Cheltenham, Victoria, 3192 Australia
Email: info@halleonard.com.au

INTRODUCTION 

To access this video and other media files, head over to www.halleonard.com/mylibrary and input the code found on page 1!

The 1930s were an era of significant evolution for the guitar. In America, blues and jazz would begin to undergo a revolution in sound, composition, and arrangements due to the commercial development of the electric guitar. In France, the appearance of Gypsy jazz as a cultural mash-up of eclectic Gypsy music and American swing jazz led to a unique style of virtuoso guitar techniques played on acoustic instruments. Gypsies are unique among peoples, never identifying themselves with a territory or having a tradition of an ancient homeland from which their ancestors migrated. In addition, they claim no right to national sovereignty in any of the lands where they reside. However, they would always absorb musical forms from whatever culture to which they were exposed and then improvise and adapt it to their style. This was never truer than when Django Reinhardt, the genius fountainhead of Gypsy jazz, heard the recordings of the legends of prewar jazz.

In fact, Gypsy jazz guitar is a great entry point to the study of improvisation. Additionally, one might hear hints of melodies, harmonies, and rhythms of many cultures. To internalize the full extent of the music and acquire the technical ability to play it requires expert guidance and study. Look no further than Gypsy jazz guitar master Jeff Magidson. He will lead you confidently through a logical course of study into the deepest recesses of classic jazz guitar music. The result will be musical knowledge and ability to last a lifetime of listening, learning, and playing.

–Dave Rubin

ACKNOWLEDGMENTS AND DEDICATION

Thanks to Paul Mehling, Evan Price, and all the members of The Hot Club of San Francisco, past and present.

This book is dedicated to my teachers, not only the ones I've had in person, but also those whose books I've purchased, or whose videos I've watched. I'm old enough to remember trying to transcribe licks off a vinyl record. Instructional books and videos were hard to come by back then. Today, there are so many resources available it's astounding. Indeed, there has never been a time when we've had access to so much knowledge, literally at our fingertips. Don't be fooled though: the virtual world can't replace a one-on-one experience. I learned more by jamming with Daniel Givone for five minutes than from any video. Not that books and videos are useless (otherwise I wouldn't have gone through the trouble of writing this one)—they are great tools for learning the grammar and vocabulary of the language at your own speed.

–Jeff Magidson

ABOUT THIS BOOK

I've purchased my share of instructional books over the years. Too often, the same scenario would play out: I would walk out of the store full of excitement and resolve, but a week later, the book would be on a shelf collecting dust. I came to realize that my issue with these books was rarely with the content and more with the delivery. Some were full of dauntingly long transcriptions that would take me days to get through. Others were full of exercises and licks, but they never seemed to get to the practical side of actually playing. In this book, I've tried to bridge the gap, keeping the exercises short enough that you won't have to spend an entire afternoon learning them, but long enough to provide context. Most are presented as eight-measure "mini solos" based on chord changes from standards in the repertoire.

The goal of this book is to introduce you to the Gypsy jazz style and provide you with the skills you need to feel comfortable in a jam situation. There are two main sections: the first on rhythm playing and the second, much longer, on soloing. Don't make the mistake of glossing over the rhythm chapter. Developing your chops as an accompanist is not only an important skill in itself—it will also greatly inform your improvisations.

In the rhythm section (no pun intended), you'll learn the common chords used in the Gypsy style and how to play La Pompe rhythm, as well as the Gypsy bossa, bolero, and waltz. The solo examples at the end of the book contain alternate voicings to help you broaden your chord vocabulary.

his bent and paralyzed ring and pinky fingers rendered virtually useless except for some chord forms. Most amazingly, he developed phenomenal, single-note chops with just his index and middle fingers. Finally, in the spring of 1930, he was able to leave the hospital.

The Early 1930s

In 1931, Django scored a job playing jazz in a club which featured African-American violinist Eddie South headlining. Hearing jazz played on the violin as he alternated sets would be an unforgettable experience. Django and his guitarist brother Joseph would soon record eight sides for the Gramophone label with bassist Louis Vola's band.

Obviously, Django was in the wrong place the night of his caravan fire, but clearly, his luck was changing. A painter named Emile Savitry heard the brothers and introduced them to the records of Duke Ellington, Joe Venuti (backed by jazz guitar pioneer Eddie Lang), and most significantly, Louis Armstrong. It was all new to Django, and he was transfixed, especially by the free-flowing improvisation of Armstrong compared to the composed jazz of Ellington.

The Early Prewar Years

Despite his numerous eccentricities and Gypsy customs foreign to the French and others, Django was able to advance his fledgling career through those who recognized his brilliance. In 1931, a group of French jazz enthusiasts formed the world's first jazz club which came to be known as the Hot Club and the guitarist would go on to be featured in their concerts.

In the summer of 1934, both Django and violinist Stephane Grappelli were coincidentally playing in a large ensemble in a café in Paris. A chance encounter behind the bandstand one day between sets resulted in the two musicians jamming extemporaneously and exuberantly with obvious rapport. As both were more interested in playing improvised jazz than polite café music, it became an opportunity they would take whenever possible.

Le Quintette du Hot Club de France

The jams continued for months throughout Paris with a quartet of Django, Grappelli, bassist Louis Vola, and rhythm guitarist Roger Chaput. When Django expressed his unhappiness with only having Chaput providing accompaniment for his solos while Grappelli enjoyed two guitars, it was agreed to bring in Joseph. In 1934, Django got to meet his idol, Louis Armstrong, and he actually jammed with the jazz titan, resulting in encouragement from the American legend. Successful concerts for the quintet organized by the Hot Club generated attention, and eventually, the future legendary name of Le Quintette du Hot Club de France was bestowed on the group. The small Ultraphone label decided to give the group a modest opportunity and "Dinah," "Tiger Rag," "Lady Be Good," and "I Saw Stars" were recorded. Throughout, Django provides buoyant, propulsive and inventive accompaniment, indicative of his eventually unmatched fretboard skills.

1936–1939: Swing Time

In 1936 and beyond, work was intermittent, lacking remuneration to match the group's growing critical acclaim. The always unpredictable nature and behavior of Django did not help, as he was often late (if he showed up at all) without a guitar, extra strings, or even a plectrum. In addition, there was his never-ending jealousy and financial conflicts with Grappelli. On top of that, Joseph, with his own simmering resentment, decided he had enough of being his brother's keeper, responsible for carrying and caring for his guitar, while concurrently having his own talents neglected. The two literally came to blows on New Year's Eve and the quintet would not be active again until the spring of 1937 when 18 sides were recorded over several days. Included were two spectacular unaccompanied Django compositions, "Improvisation" and "Parfum," which remain landmarks to this day.

In early 1939, the Hot Club moved into new quarters and, fortuitously, the Duke Ellington Orchestra arrived in time for its opening. While in Paris, Ellington was treated to an exclusive performance by the quintet, during which he and Django jammed. Before they parted, plans were made to get together in New York. With Ellington still in Paris, an impromptu recording session was arranged for Django to play with trumpeter Rex Stewart and others from the orchestra. Though Stewart was dubious at first, after hearing Django in a guitar battle with Henri Salvador and Oscar Aleman, he was convinced.

A tour of England and Europe was inaugurated in the summer of 1939, but with Hitler's blitzkrieg looming, the quintet could not get beyond London or complete those engagements. Thinking he would be safe at home, Django went back to Paris in a panic, leaving his belongings in the hotel room, including his guitar. Grappelli stayed behind in what would become the end of the original Le Quintette du Hot Club de Paris.

The War Years

Paradoxically, the war years in occupied Paris were a boon to jazz and Django. The French, as well as other Europeans, responded to the joys and sorrows expressed in the music. Ironically, even the Nazis enjoyed hearing Django in the cabarets. His response was to compose one of his enduring classics, "Nuages," its melancholy melody becoming an anthem and temporary balm to the French people. Paradoxically, the Nazi's hypocrisy flew in the face of Hitler's tirades against the music he called an American-Judeo-Negro conspiracy. Alongside the genocide of European Jews and other people groups deemed "undesirable" by the Third Reich in the Holocaust, Gypsies would be rounded up and exterminated by the hundreds of thousands to "purify" the German "Aryan" race. In addition, where many jazz clubs only booked black jazz artists in the past, they now welcomed French musicians as the Americans left for home, fearing for their lives.

When liberation finally came in the summer of 1944, Django found he was well-known to the American military stationed in Paris. Jams with members of the Glenn Miller Band resulted in recordings being made under the name Jazz Club of Francais. Contributing to his legend was the story of Miller pianist Mel Powell swapping choruses with Django until he closed the lid on his piano and just listened to the virtuosic Gypsy improvise. The interaction with so many "Yanks" through 1945 and beyond only inflamed his long simmering desire to go to the U.S., while playing his amplified Selmer and amp foretold things to come.

Reunion

In the fall of 1945, Stephane Grappelli called from London and spoke with Django for the first time in six years, resulting in the guitarist and family minus Joseph making the journey across the Channel in early 1946. Unfortunately, Django took ill soon after arriving, necessitating an operation followed by a cancelled tour and his forced return to Paris while Grappelli once again remained behind. Back in Montmartre, Django discovered very little work as one club after another had closed. Lacking ambition, he fell into a state of near atrophy, with only his new quest to be a painter seeming to hold his attention. Previous plans to write a film score were sabotaged by his irresponsible behavior and lack of music reading. However, booking arrangements were underway to allow him to go to America.

The New World and Touring with Duke Ellington

On October 29, 1946, Django arrived in New York, without so much as luggage or a toothbrush, to begin a last-minute, 21-city tour with the Duke Ellington Orchestra. Additionally, he did not even bring his beloved Selmer Modele Jazz, mistakenly thinking his great fame would have spread across the Atlantic with guitar companies clamoring to provide him with instruments. In addition, his attraction to the glamour of Hollywood convinced him he would be in films and meet movie stars (indeed, Dorothy Lamour was a big fan). Alas, none of these naïve dreams would be forthcoming.

Duke had been duly impressed with Django when they met and played together in Paris. However, he seemed to have had little or no time to rehearse or to plan how Django could best be presented. The guitarist's vaunted ability at being able to "pick" immediately on anything he heard saved most of the performances, despite his inability to convey his choice of keys. However, his distaste for the relatively heavy Gibson ES-300 and amp provided for his use, as well as his chronic lateness, also contributed to the whole affair being dubbed a failure upon conclusion. Les Paul, who was significantly influenced by Django, befriended him to a degree, which would later carry over to his going well out of his way for the Gypsy's family.

Two of the last dates were at Carnegie Hall in late November, where he arrived unconscionably late for the second performance, with the end coming in Detroit in early December where he was said to have "stolen the show." Audiences often went wild, demanding several encores, and guitarists flocked to see him. Potential work in California with Tommy Dorsey's band failed to materialize, and he was reportedly approached by Benny Goodman to join his combo, which he turned down, ever fearful he would not be the star. During down time, he set up painting in his hotel room, apparently enticing women to come up and pose nude for him. Tired, homesick, and missing his family, on February 13, 1947, Django returned to Paris disappointed but inspired by the new American bebop jazz being played in New York.

1947–1953: Back Home

Through to 1953, Django would make many quintet recordings, including with Grappelli when in Paris. The quintet with the violinist would perform regularly at the ABC music hall in Paris from late 1947 to early 1948, with Django displaying some of his old passion and improvisational creativity. In actuality, he was devoting more time to painting in his apartment studio. During one of their latter dates, Dizzy Gillespie, who happened to be in Paris with his big band, stopped by Django's dressing room and the two jammed.

In early 1949, Django and Grappelli toured Italy with an Italian rhythm section. While in Rome, Django learned Benny Goodman would be arriving from Paris, and he made it a point to greet him at the train station and to attend a rehearsal.

Again, Goodman invited him to come back to the U.S. with him, or at least play with the band at their concert. Django accepted the invitation to sit in but then failed to show up.

Back in Paris, Django once again hung up his guitar in his caravan and seldom played it. Though out of the limelight, he was not forgotten by musicians. In early 1951, he made a bit of a comeback with an extended Paris club engagement which found him the star in the company of much younger jazz musicians. When pushed to it, he could still play with astounding improvisational force and was happy to be playing different music.

In the fall, he retired to north central France. There, he indulged his passion for fishing and billiards. Occasionally, he would make the trek to Paris for a rare broadcast or recording session. In early 1952, he took his current quintet to Brussels and played a concert sponsored by the Hot Club de Belgique. The audience was indifferent, though—not because time had passed Django by, but because he was playing too modern and progressive, enhanced by the volume of his amplified guitar. Ironically, as his playing advanced remarkably, bebop was on the wane in the U.S., which his European audiences had never caught up with anyway.

A Planned Second Act

Despite disappointments, offers still came his way. In early 1953, while playing an engagement at The Ringside (boxer Sugar Ray Robinson's Parisian club), he saw Jazz at the Philharmonic organizer, Norman Granz. Django had previously met the American impresario in New York during his 1946 tour and was offered a spot on a JATP tour of Europe, the U.S., and Japan for the fall. He readily agreed. Granz set up a recording session in March as promotion and a 10-inch LP titled *The Great Artistry of Django Reinhardt* was released. Eager to show he had much more music in him, he displayed complete confidence with his electric guitar and phenomenal talent. Plans were also hatched to record the concerts and for Django to be in the studio later with his touring rhythm section augmented by pianist Oscar Peterson and bassist Ray Brown.

In April, he recorded his fourth session for Decca Records. Containing only four songs and backed by a modern ensemble, the results were Django at his most introspective, economic, and assured. They would be his last recordings.

In May, he played a series of dates in Switzerland. While there, he started having severe headaches, but ignored them. When his fingers became stiff, his wife urged him to see a doctor, but his experience after the fire left him with a fear of medical procedures.

Returning to France, he learned Bing Crosby had come looking for him. "Der Bingle" was hoping to entice him to tour the U.S. in a duo similar to what he once had with Eddie Lang. Ever the fatalist, Django accepted his bad luck and looked forward to touring with Jazz at the Philharmonic in a few months. It was not to be. On the morning of May 16, 1953 after getting up and walking to his favorite bistro for a cup of tea, he collapsed and died of a cerebral hemorrhage later in the afternoon. He was 43.

Epilogue

Les Paul willingly spent more time with Django than any other guitarist. He idolized him and there was mutual admiration. Unfortunately, when the Gypsy legend died, he left his wife Naguine virtually penniless. In the Gypsy tradition, a fire was set to destroy all of their belongings, including Django's Selmer guitar. Naguine did not possess even one of his records and moved her caravan back to the zone. When Les and Mary Ford were in Paris, they went in search of her, only to find her living in squalor without heat or electricity. After seeing her plight, Les convinced the record companies to give her back royalties to the tune of $10,000. He also bought her clothes, along with a phonograph and as many of Django's records as he could hunt down. Additionally, Les had a gravestone erected in Samois, France.

Gypsy Jazz After Django

Between Django's passing and 1980, his contemporaries and a younger generation of guitarists kept playing Gypsy jazz in Europe and, occasionally, with American jazz musicians. That year, 13-year-old Alsatian prodigy, Bireli Lagrene, recorded *Routes to Django*, and a new flag bearer arrived to make the music vital again. Joseph wept when he heard it, exclaiming he was "Django born again." Besides his worldwide acclaim as a spectacular new guitar hero, Lagrene opened the way for Angelo Debarre, Stochelo Rosenberg, Gonzolo Bergara, Tchavalo Schmitt, Romane, Fapy Lafertin, Nous'che Rosenberg, Joscho Stephan, Adrien Moignard, and Hono Winterstein, among others. In addition, at the beginning of 2000, two of Django's grandsons, David Reinhardt and Dallas Baumgartner, began performing.

Today, the "children" of Django may be heard at Gypsy jazz festivals from France to New York and beyond, as well as in countless clubs. Perhaps most significant is the way Gypsies in France, Belgium, the Netherlands, and Germany now teach their children to honor Django by learning his songs note-for-note.

Classic Gear and Set Up

Gypsy jazz can be played on any style guitar. At the end of his career, Django played an electric guitar, as do many of the masters of the style today. That being said, the traditional Gypsy jazz sound comes from the Selmer Maccaferri-style guitars. (Maccaferri was the luthier who came up with the original design, and Selmer was the manufacturer.) Unlike a typical acoustic, these guitars have either a small, oval sound hole ("petite bouche") or a wide, D-shaped one ("grande bouche"). They have a distinctive, mid-range sound that some describe as "nasal" and is immediately recognizable as "that Gypsy sound." The ideal strings are silver-plated copper on a steel core, and the leading manufacture is Savarez. To get optimal volume, the action should be set higher than on your average steel string. If there's not enough tension, the instrument won't fully respond. Regarding plectrums, it's best to use thicker picks of at least 1.5mm.

Django Reinhardt's Selmer #503

Photo courtesy of Collections Musíc de la musique/Cliché Albert Giordan D.R.

CHAPTER 2

RHYTHM 

The rhythm guitar is the backbone of Gypsy jazz, and one cannot stress its importance enough. With a dual harmonic and percussive function, it supplies the canvas on which the soloists paint their picture. In traditional Gypsy jazz formations, there are no drums. Keeping time (maintaining the tempo) is primarily the responsibility of the rhythm guitarist, and anyone who aspires to play in the style must first reach a level of proficiency in "the rhythm chair."

This may seem off-putting initially, as we are all impatient to learn some of Django's two-fingered magic tricks, but know that this is the path. Most people spend years playing rhythm before becoming lead players. Some, like Hono Winterstein or Nous'che Rosenberg, devote their entire careers to it.

I spent ten years as a rhythm guitarist with the Hot Club of San Francisco, one of the premier Gypsy jazz bands in the U.S. I came to know much of the repertoire inside and out, not only learning the basic chord changes to the tunes, but all the alternate voicings available as well. Of course, I tried to hone my lead chops on the side. Who could resist? One day, I had a flash of insight and remembered something one of my first teachers had told me: "Your soloing is only as good as your rhythm playing." I had assumed he meant that one needed to develop a good sense of time by playing rhythm. Now, I realized that it wasn't just the tempo or groove he was talking about. One also needed to develop a rich chord vocabulary. Improvising in the Gypsy jazz style (and jazz in general, for that matter) is largely based on chord forms. The more voicings you know of a chord, the more ammunition you can use to solo over it. I discovered that all those years playing in the rhythm chair had given me the perfect foundation for my lead playing.

Gypsy Jazz Chords

Since Django's band was playing without amplification, they sought to play the fullest chords possible. Keeping this in mind, you need to choose what chord voicings you use, according to context. Now that most guitars are amplified, these thicker chords can sound muddy. The goal is to supply the harmony without taking up too much room and overpowering the soloist. Sometimes, a simple, three-note chord will be more appropriate. In other situations where you need more volume, you might want to play a chord containing five or six notes. In the following pages, you will find the most common chords used in Gypsy jazz. Try to become familiar with all of them. Your knowledge of these chords will make it easier to understand and learn the licks later in the book.

Chord Legend

■ = Root
□ = Root Absent from Voicing
T = Thumb

Major Chords

C

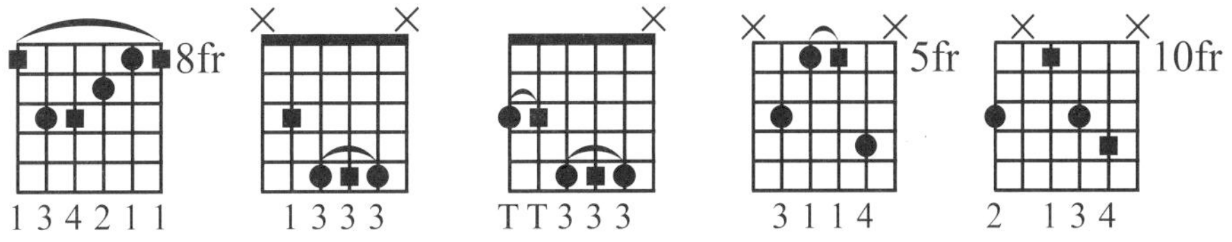

8fr 1 3 4 2 1 1 | 1 3 3 3 | T T 3 3 3 | 5fr 3 1 1 4 | 10fr 2 1 3 4

C6

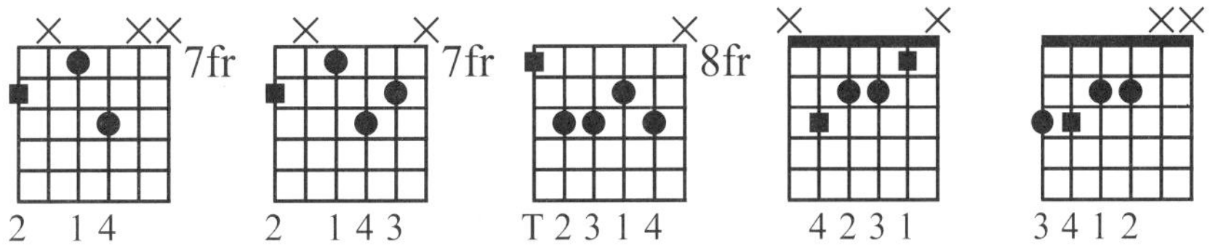

7fr 2 1 4 | 7fr 2 1 4 3 | 8fr T 2 3 1 4 | 4 2 3 1 | 3 4 1 2

C^{6}_{9}

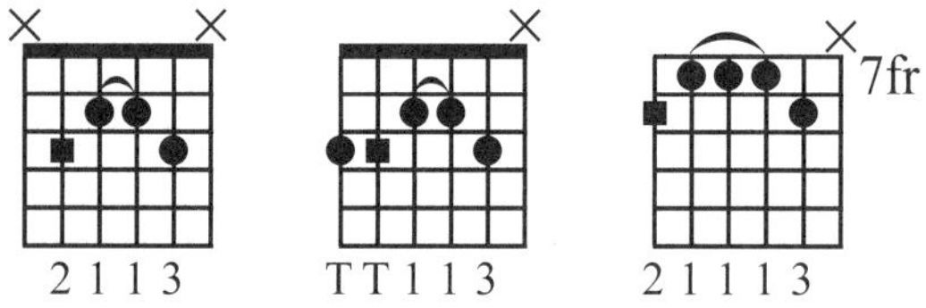

2 1 1 3 | T T 1 1 3 | 7fr 2 1 1 1 3

Cmaj7

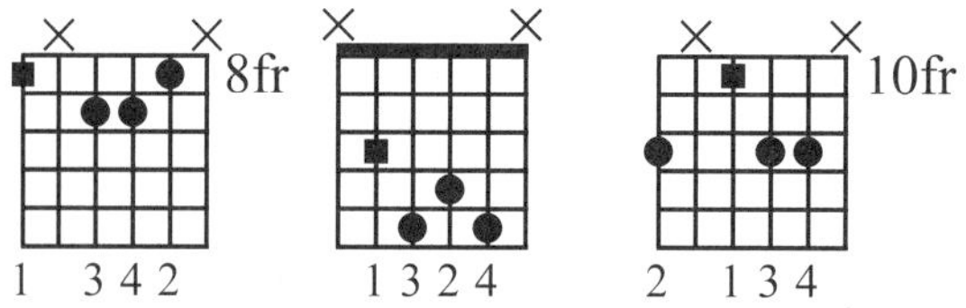

8fr 1 3 4 2 | 1 3 2 4 | 10fr 2 1 3 4

Cmaj9

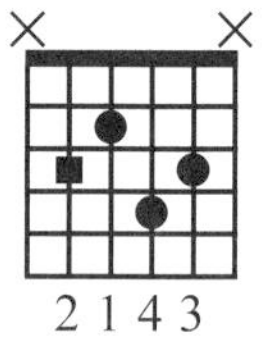

2 1 4 3

Minor Chords

Cm

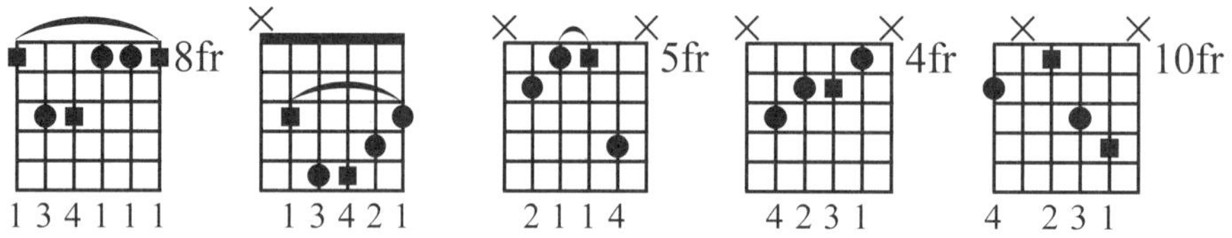

8fr 1 3 4 1 1 1 | 1 3 4 2 1 | 5fr 2 1 1 4 | 4fr 4 2 3 1 | 10fr 4 2 3 1

Cm6

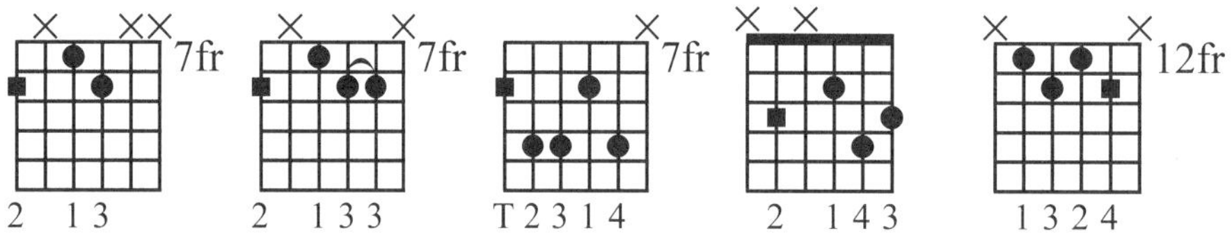

7fr 2 1 3 | 7fr 2 1 3 3 | 7fr T 2 3 1 4 | 2 1 4 3 | 12fr 1 3 2 4

Cm7

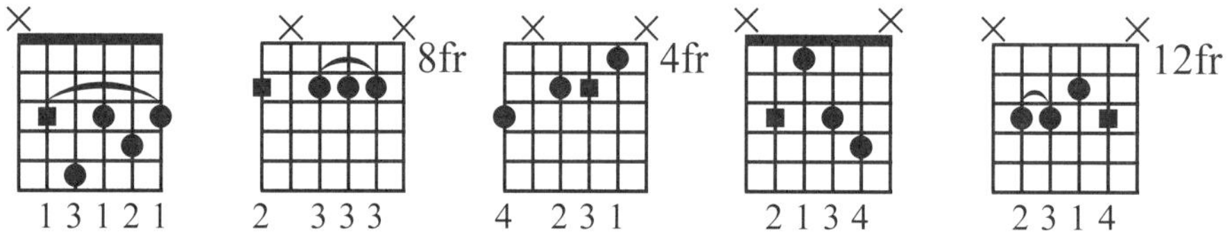

1 3 1 2 1 | 8fr 2 3 3 3 | 4fr 4 2 3 1 | 2 1 3 4 | 12fr 2 3 1 4

Cm9

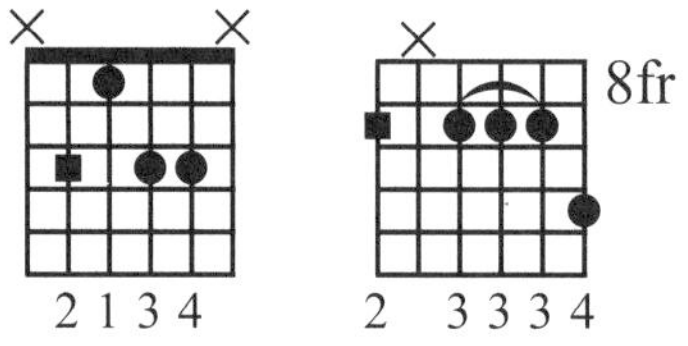

2 1 3 4 | 8fr 2 3 3 3 4

Cm(maj7)

1 4 2 3 1 | 7fr 2 3 4 1 | 8fr T 3 2 1 1

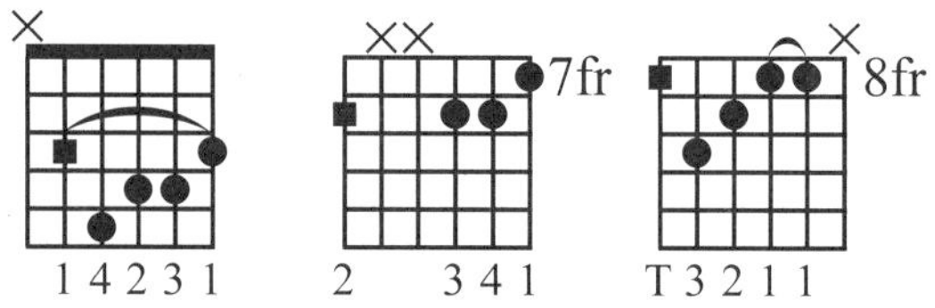

Minor 7♭5 Chords

Cm7♭5

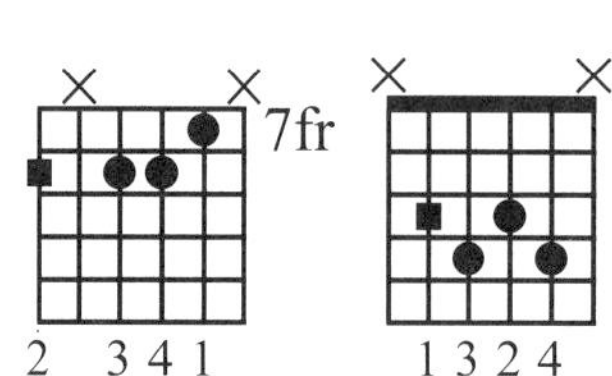

Dominant 7 Chords

C7

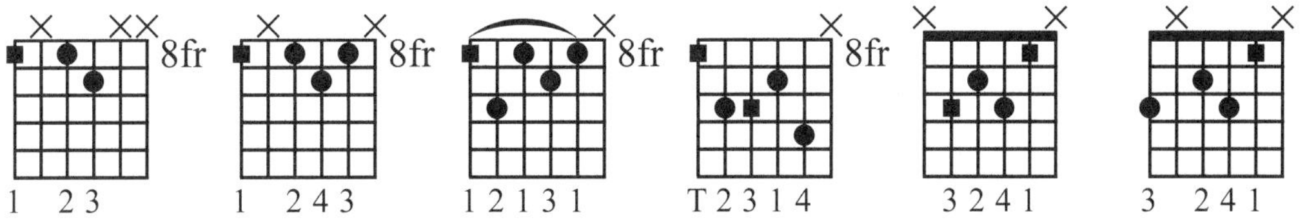

8fr 1 2 3

8fr 1 2 4 3

8fr 1 2 1 3 1

8fr T 2 3 1 4

3 2 4 1

3 2 4 1

C13

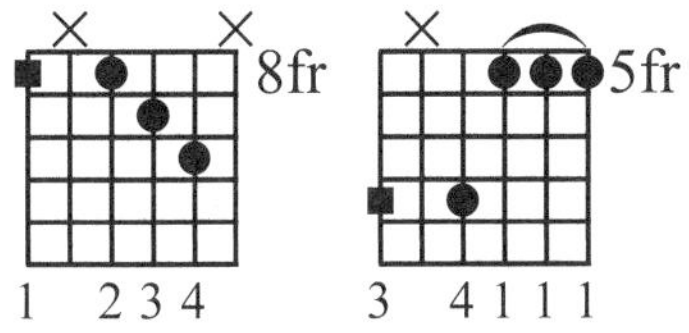

8fr 1 2 3 4

5fr 3 4 1 1 1

C9

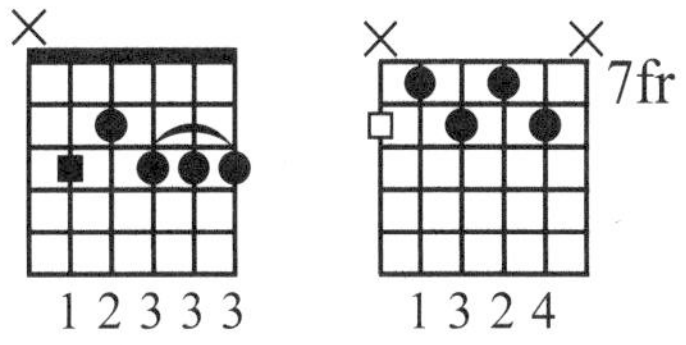

1 2 3 3 3

7fr 1 3 2 4

C^{9}_{13}

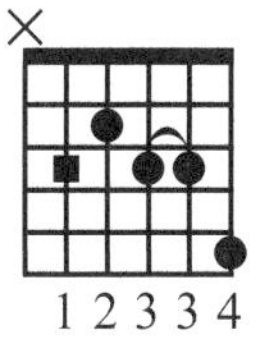

1 2 3 3 4

C7♭9

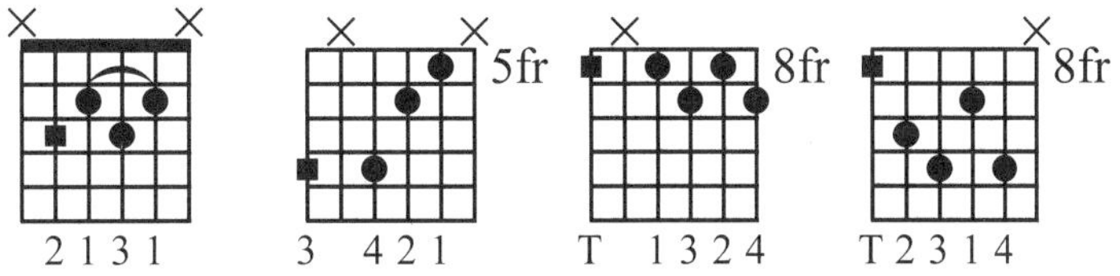

2 1 3 1

5fr 3 4 2 1

8fr T 1 3 2 4

8fr T 2 3 1 4

C7♯9

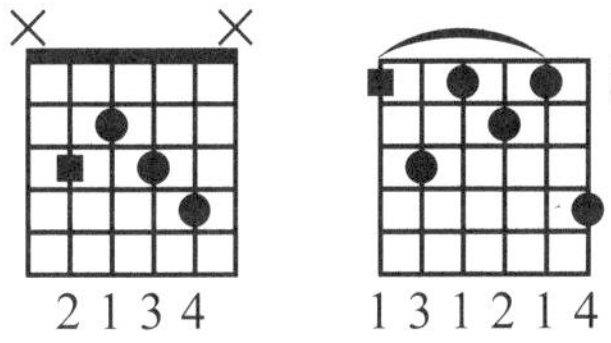

2 1 3 4

8fr 1 3 1 2 1 4

C7♯5

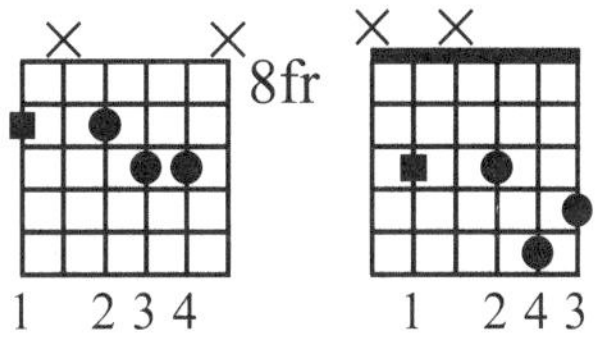

8fr 1 2 3 4

1 2 4 3

$C7^{\sharp 5}_{\flat 9}$

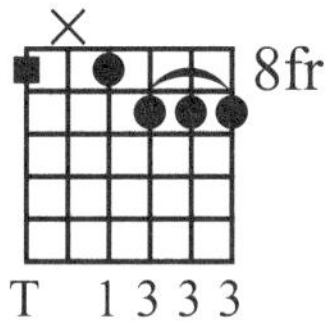

8fr T 1 3 3 3

C7♭5

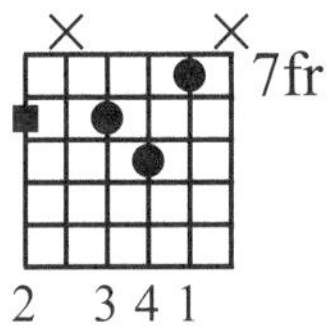

7fr 2 3 4 1

C9♭5

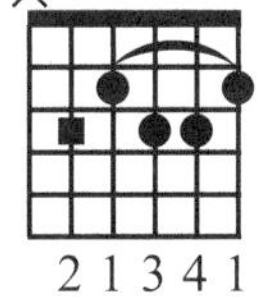

2 1 3 4 1

C13(♭9)

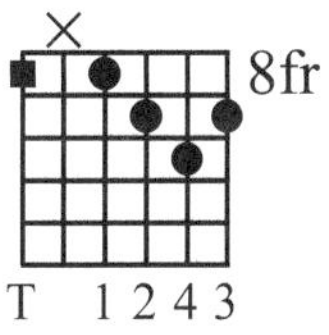

8fr T 1 2 4 3

C13/D♭

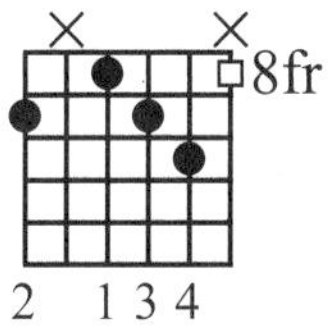

8fr 2 1 3 4

Diminished 7 Chords

C°7

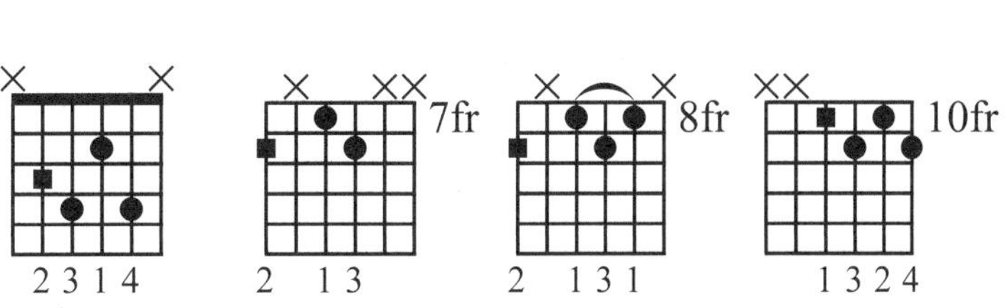

Right-Hand Technique

The right-hand technique in Gypsy jazz is quite different than in other styles. Whereas many electric guitarists learn to play with their wrist anchored on the bridge, in Gypsy jazz, the wrist is slightly bent and floats above it. This bent-wrist position can deliver a faster, stronger pick stroke. The fact that the hand is not in contact with the body also allows for more resonance from the instrument. If you need proof that the bent wrist approach really works, try this: shake your hand, first with the wrist locked like you are holding a hammer, then with a loose wrist, like you are shaking a thermometer. You'll immediately notice how much faster the bent-wrist motion is. Be aware that this technique takes time to develop. At first, you may feel like you are regressing. Have patience and persist, and the exercises in this book will help you get there. Always play them with precision as your goal, not speed. Like many things in the learning process, the slower you go, the quicker you get there. We'll talk more about right-hand technique in Chapter 3 when we discuss lead playing.

The Pick

Most Gypsy jazz players use an extremely thick pick (around 3.5 mm). An average pick is in the neighborhood of 1 mm, so the first time you hold one might feel strange. These larger picks not only provide more volume, they also have a warmer sound. In Django's day, the Gypsies fashioned picks from all kinds of materials: plastic, bone, wood. Tortoise shell was apparently Django's preference. Gypsy picks can be hard to find at local music stores, but many are available online. The most popular manufacturer is Michael Wegen in the Netherlands (*www.wegenpicks.com*). Using one of these handmade picks isn't an absolute necessity, but I would recommend using something rigid enough that it won't bend when making contact with the string. The Dunlop 1.5 mm is a good example.

Holding the Pick

The position of the pick is slightly different in the Gypsy jazz style and might be one of the harder adjustments to make. Most of us learned to place the pick on the edge of our index finger and lock it in place with the tip of the thumb. You can start from this position then slide the pick towards the joint of the thumb. With the pick anchored against here, you'll find that you have more stability and can generate more volume.

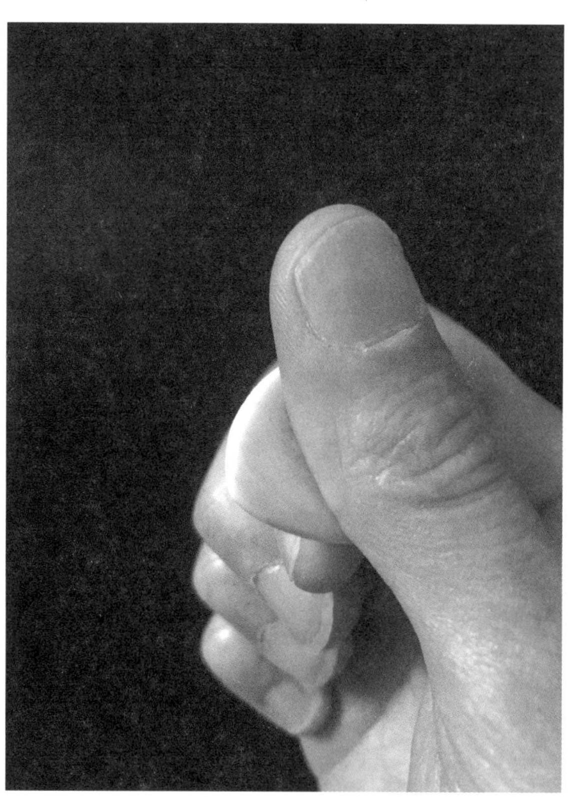

La Pompe

La Pompe (literally "the pump") is a term French musicians used to describe a rhythm alternating between the bass and treble like one would hear from the left hand in stride piano or from an accordion—whatever is providing the underlying pulse of the music. In the Gypsy jazz world, La Pompe refers to the swing rhythm played on guitar. In its essence, it is a simple quarter note rhythm, although there is a lot more going on with La Pompe than first meets the ear.

Remember that as the rhythm guitarist, you are also playing the role of the drummer. You are the one bringing the swing, and it's no small responsibility. People can, and do, argue endlessly about what swings and what doesn't. It is impossible to codify. Some people play more on the back of the beat. Some play a little more in front. Then, there is the question of the accent that occurs between the beats—the infamous "upstroke" of La Pompe. In this small space is a universe of possibilities. The accent can be loud, soft, short, long, and sometimes inaudible but still implied by the wrist movement. It becomes very subjective, and there is not one right way of playing it. In fact, the different Gypsy clans each developed their own distinctive styles. *La Hollandaise* emphasizes beats 2 and 4, *La Parisienne* emphasizes beats 1 and 3, and *l'Alsacienne* treats all four beats equally. These are, however, subtle variations, but it is not difficult to establish some basic guidelines as to what La Pompe should sound like.

The most common mistake beginners make when learning La Pompe is to accentuate the backbeat (2 and 4) too heavily. It's as if they are trying to reproduce the sound of a kick drum and a snare, which is a huge dynamic jump and sounds very lopsided. A better way to think would be the sound of a ride cymbal and a hi-hat. The hi-hat plays on beats 2 and 4, but it is not particularly louder—it just has a crisper sound. The following exercises will teach you La Pompe step by step. The video will be particularly useful for this topic.

In this exercise, use only down strokes, releasing the pressure on the strings after each stroke to stop the resonance. Be careful to mute the strings that aren't used. Only the three notes of the chord should be heard.

FIG. 1

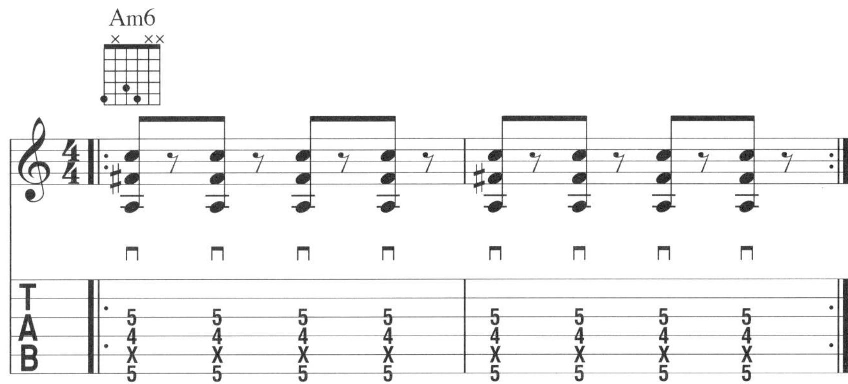

Now, we'll accentuate the second and fourth beats. It is important not to overemphasize them, however. Think of these beats as slightly shorter and crisper.

FIG. 2

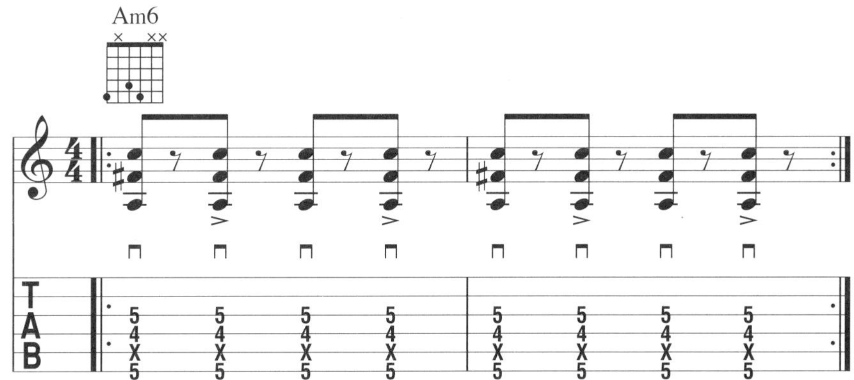

Building on these exercises, we'll now add the upstroke before beats 1 and 3. The upstroke should drag over the strings, sounding more like a short drum roll than a single hit. Refer to the video for a more in-depth explanation.

FIG. 3

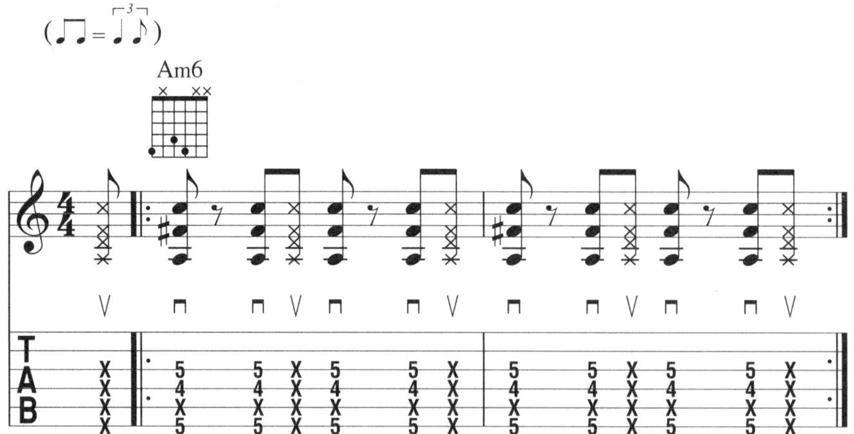

Now, we'll put this into application by playing a chord progression similar to the A section of "Minor Swing." Note that while there are three different chords, we are only using one chord form. The form starting on fret 7 functions as an E7 chord. We have simply replaced the root of the chord with the 5th. Feel free to experiment with other chord voicings as well.

FIG. 4

At slower tempos, it is common to let all four beats ring out. Though this might sound easier, it can be deceptively challenging as any fluctuation in time will be magnified. Many players will move their right hand at twice the speed in order to maintain a steady tempo. Refer to the video for a demonstration of this technique.

FIG. 5

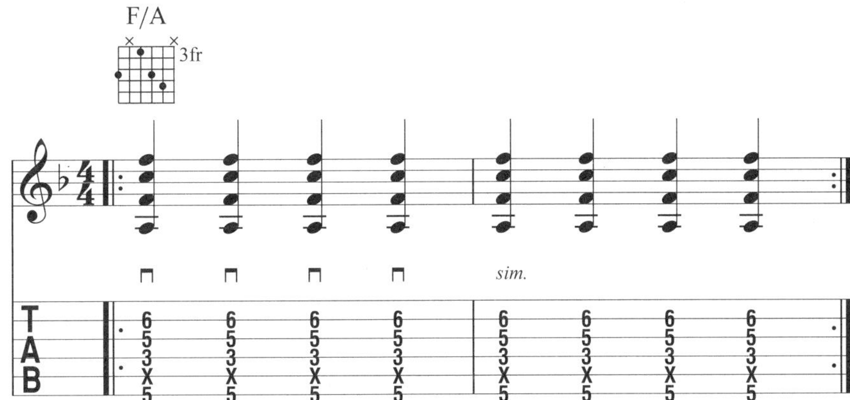

Now, we'll put this into application using a progression similar to "Nuages." Note the alternating bass notes in measures one and two, and the ascending cadence in measures 3 and 4. This cadence can be found in many Gypsy jazz tunes where you might otherwise have two measures of the same chord.

FIG. 6

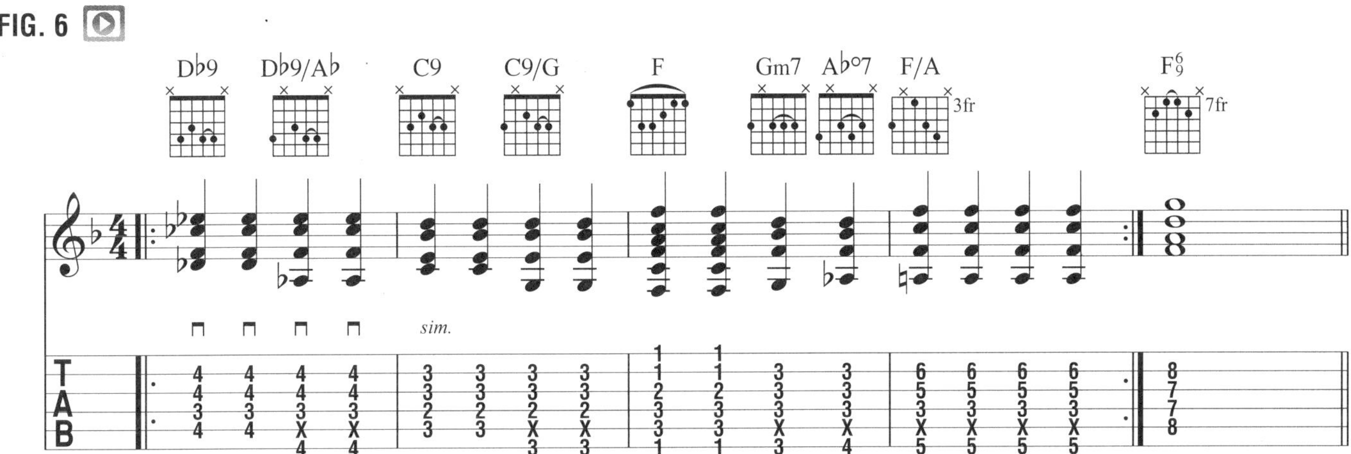

Another variation used at slow and medium tempos is to let the first and third beats ring out but choke the second and fourth. Think "long, short, long short."

FIG. 7

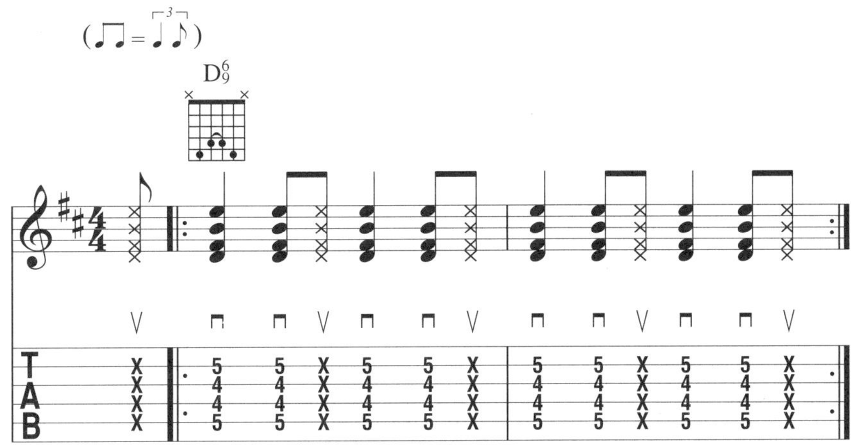

For this exercise, we'll use two measures found in songs like "Django's Castle." Note the A13/B♭ chord. Though this chord starts on the note B♭ it functions as an altered A7 chord (A7♭9 with the ♭9 as the bass note). This is an extremely common chord substitution in Gypsy jazz. It can be used on any V7 chord.

FIG. 8

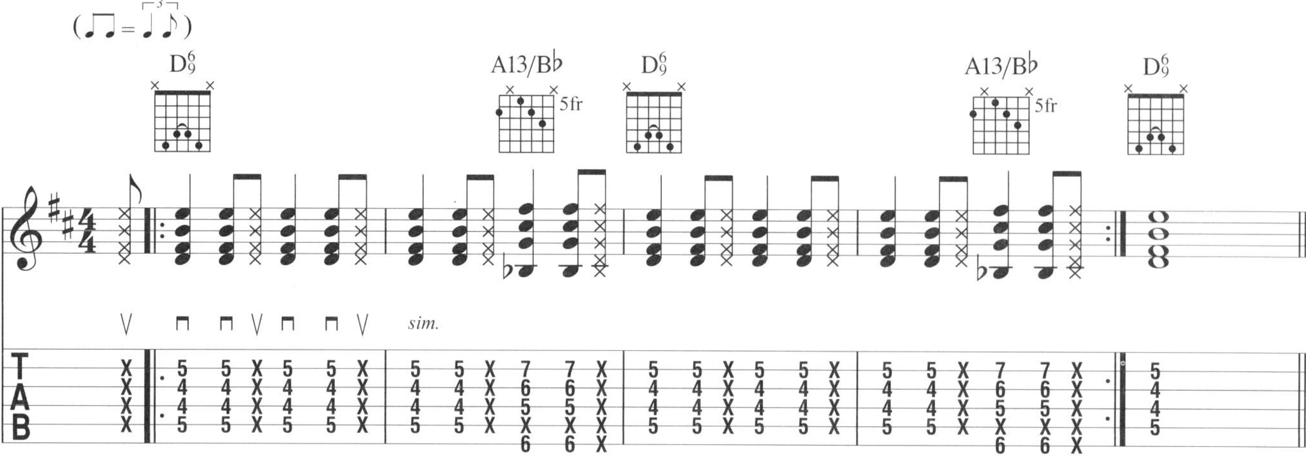

Other Rhythms

Though La Pompe may be the trademark rhythm in Gypsy jazz, it is by no means the only one. In the following, you'll learn three more must-know rhythms likely to come up at any Gypsy jazz jam session.

The Waltz Rhythm

Waltzes were a standard part of the repertoire in the Parisian dance halls where Django played his first gigs as an accompanist on the banjo. The lead instrument at the time was the accordion, which had been introduced by Italian immigrants. Soon, Django and others were transcribing the melodies played on the accordion to their stringed instruments, resulting in some of the unique ornamentations one hears in Gypsy jazz.

Though it is in 3/4 time, the waltz rhythm can be approached in much the same way as the previous exercise. But instead of an alternating "long, short, long, short" rhythm, we'll play "long, short, short, long, short, short." Note that a full barre is not used on the Em and Am chords, which are demonstrated in the following two figures. The first string is muted here to get a more compact sound.

FIG. 9

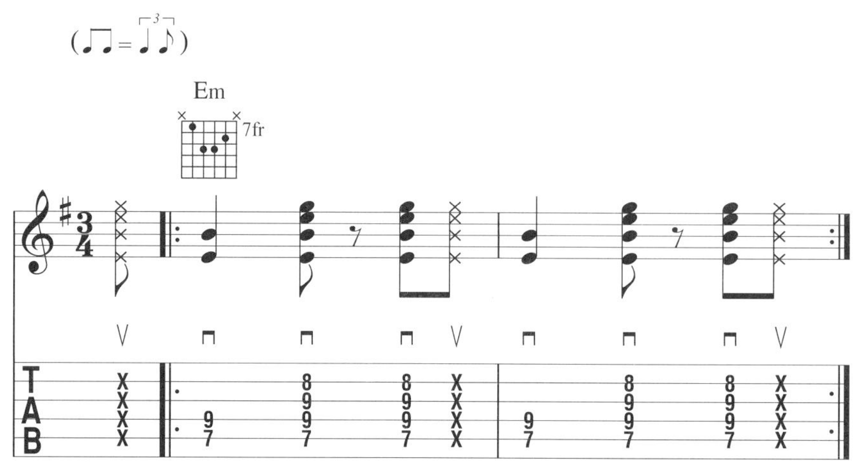

Like the blues, most waltzes follow the same form. The difference is they are much longer with several different sections. The good news is that once you've learned one, you'll find the others come much easier. For this exercise, we'll use a typical waltz progression.

FIG. 10 

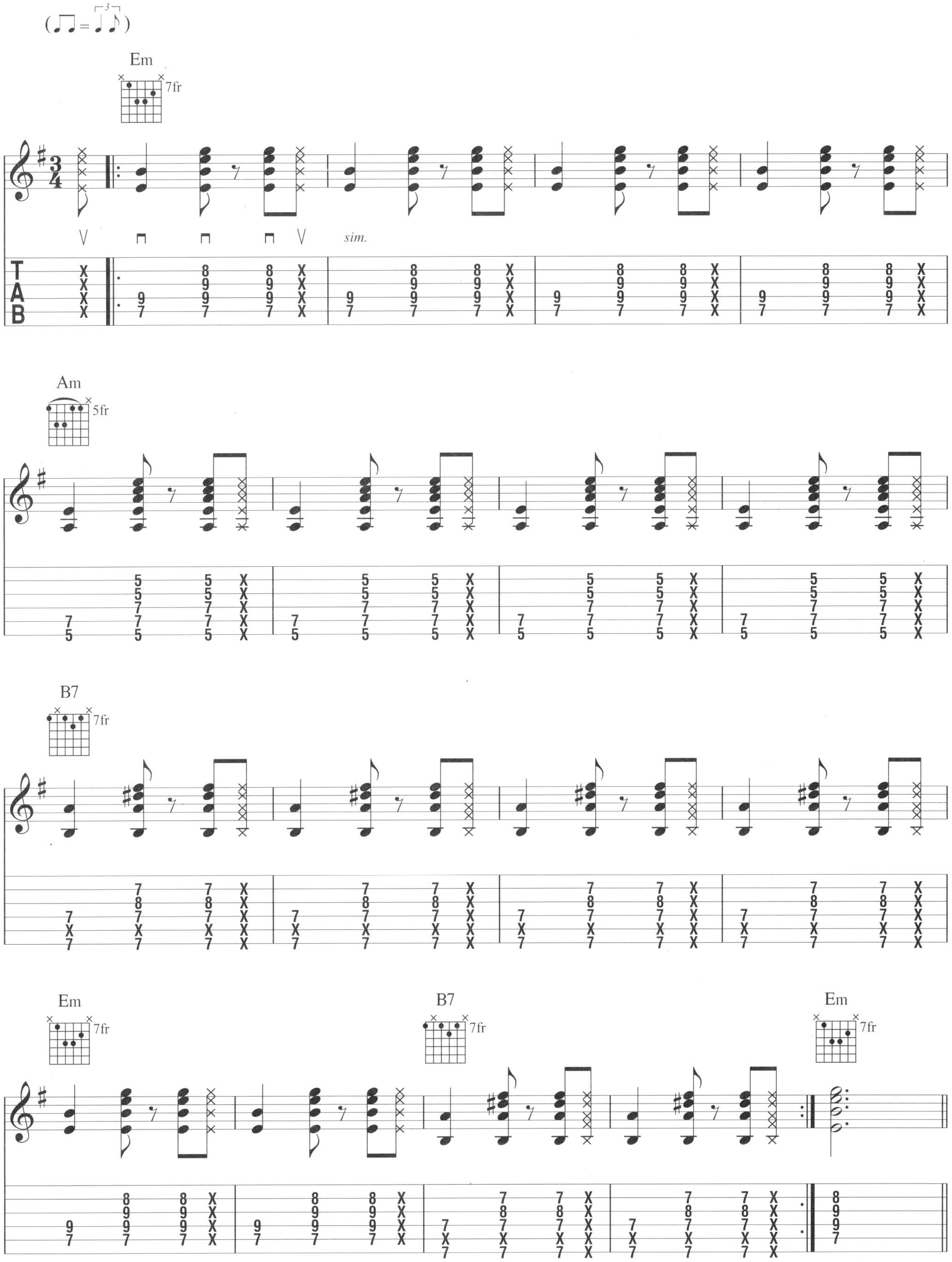

Em Am B7 Em B7 Em

sim.

The Bossa Rhythm

Django passed away in 1953, but Gypsy jazz continued to evolve, assimilating new rhythms into the repertoire. The *Gypsy bossa* is a perfect example. It was popularized by Stochelo Rosenberg, notably in his recording of the song "Bossa Dorado," written by Dorado Schmitt.

The Gypsy bossa is a more modern rhythm. The right-hand pattern can be found in many pop songs, in fact. Pay close attention to the anticipated chord changes that occur on the last eighth note of each measure.

FIG. 11

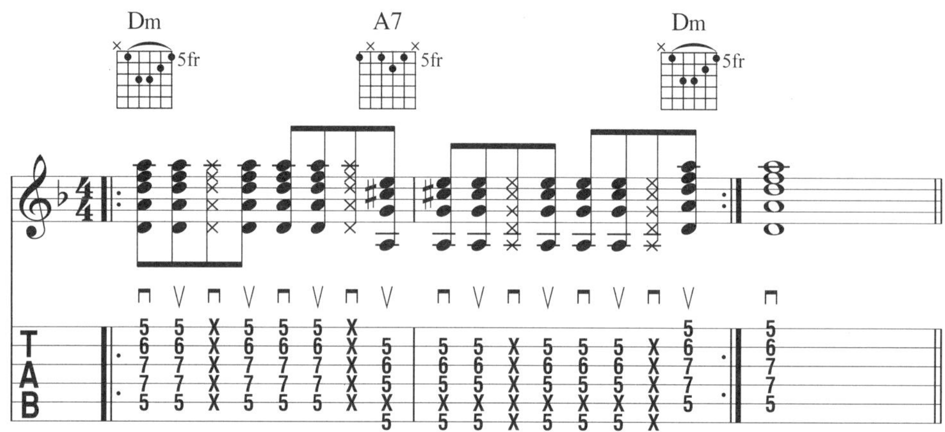

To put this into application, we'll play a progression similar to the A section of "Bossa Dorado."

FIG. 12

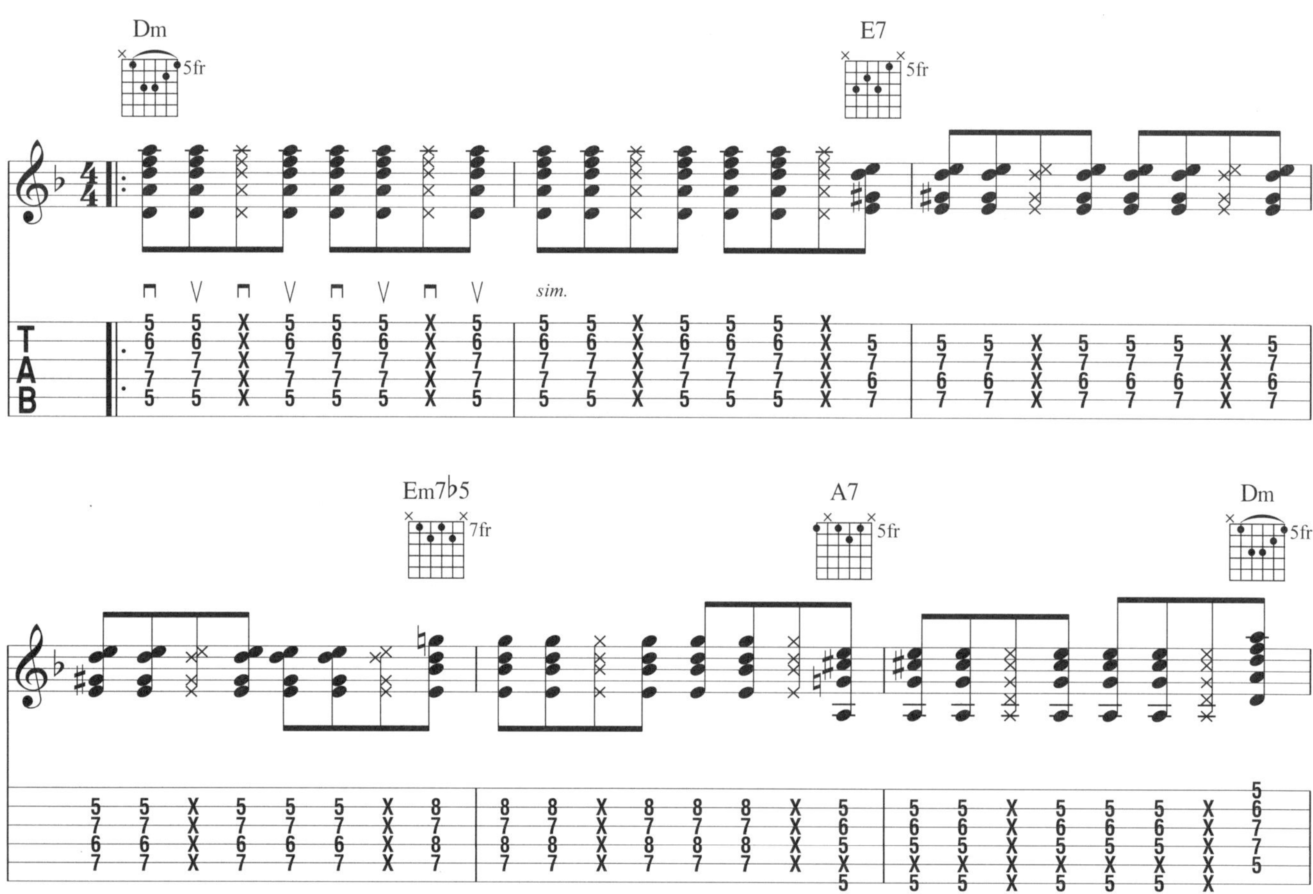

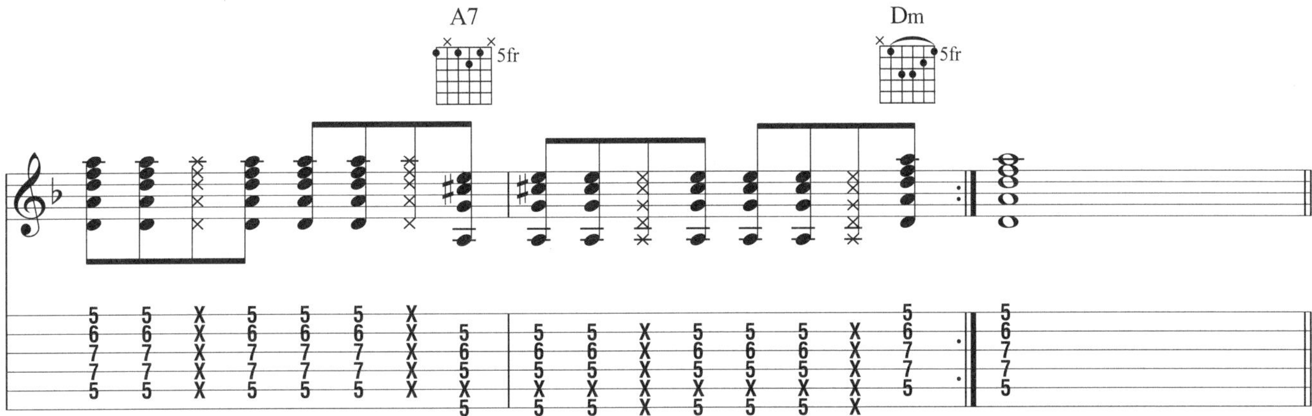

The Bolero Rhythm

The *bolero* originated in Spain, but the version played in Gypsy jazz is closer to the bolero rhythm played in Cuba and Latin America. The most popular piece using this rhythm is Django's "Troublant Bolero," another must-know in the repertoire. Since this rhythm is somewhat complex, we will learn it in two steps. In this first exercise, we'll become familiar with the basic pulse.

FIG. 13

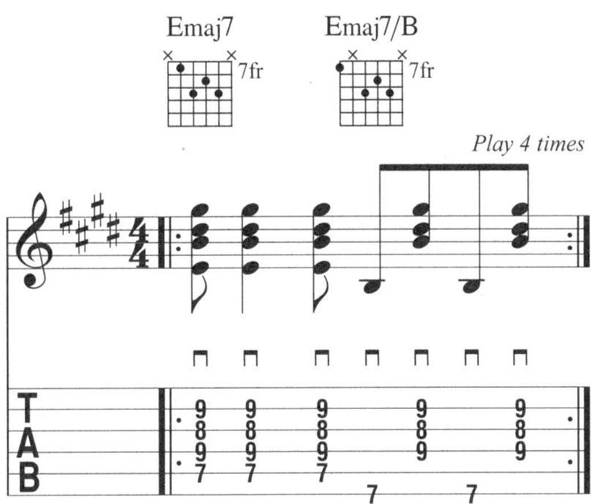

Building on that, we'll break the second eighth note into a 16th-note triplet to get the complete rhythm. Don't hesitate to consult the video, as this is one of the trickier right-hand techniques.

FIG. 14

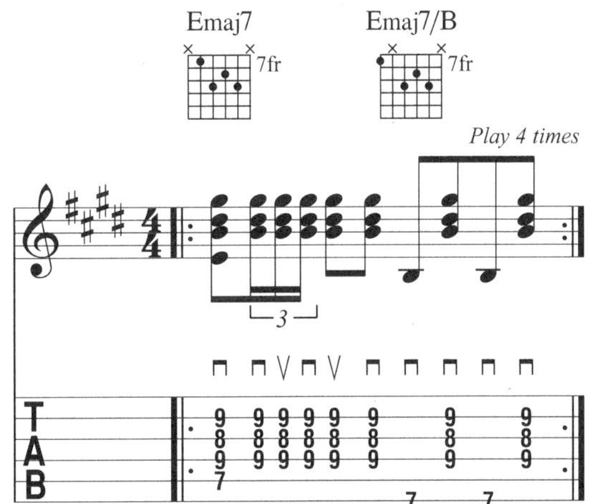

Now, we'll put this into application using a chord progression similar to the A section of "Troublant Bolero."

FIG. 15

Before moving on to the next chapter of this book, I would encourage you to play along with all the provided practice tracks, located on page 92. Try using all the different voicings from the "chords" section. Remember: "Your soloing is only as good as your rhythm playing."

CHAPTER 3

MECHANICS OF PLAYING

Picking

The Rest Stroke

The *rest stroke* is the key to playing fast with clarity and probably the hardest technique to master. Some say Django developed this style playing the banjo, but there is evidence that it may be related to other stringed instruments that the Gypsies would have been familiar with, like the Turkish oud or Greek bouzouki. Classical guitarists use a similar technique called *apoyando*, though they use their thumb instead of a pick.

The concept is to use the weight of the hand to strike the string much like a hammer striking a nail. The wrist initiates the movement, and the weight of the "hammer" drives the "nail" in. After striking the string, the pick stops, or rests on the string below. The result is a more forceful stroke with less tension.

We learned in Chapter 2 on rhythm that the right hand should float above the top of the guitar. When strumming, this is fairly natural. When playing single notes, however, it's a different story. I know I found this extremely awkward at first. I was used to having my palm on the bridge to give me a sense of position. Now, it felt like I had no control. I eventually learned that most Gypsy jazz players use their fingers to find that sense of position, either by posting their pinky on the top of the guitar or uncurling their fingers and letting them gently brush over it. This adjustment changed everything. Now, my wrist movement had speed and control.

Another important aspect that eluded me for months was the role of the elbow, regarding string position. When you move from one string to another, the whole forearm changes position, and when playing on one string, it is all wrist motion. Imagine your arm like that of a drill machine in a factory. The elbow joint is the fulcrum, moving the arm up and down to various positions where the wrist joint drill is activated.

Proper Position

1. The right hand should be detached from the body of the guitar.
2. The wrist is slightly bent, allowing freer movement.
3. The pick should strike halfway between the bridge and the sound hole.
4. The pick is perpendicular to the string but has a forward slant.

Raise the pick about an inch above the string, and let it fall through with the pick coming to rest on the string below. When playing the high E string, let the pick fall on the top of the guitar.

FIG. 16

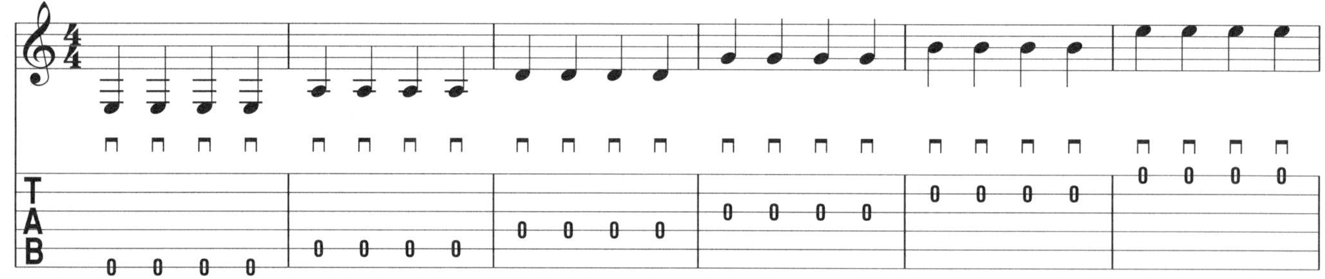

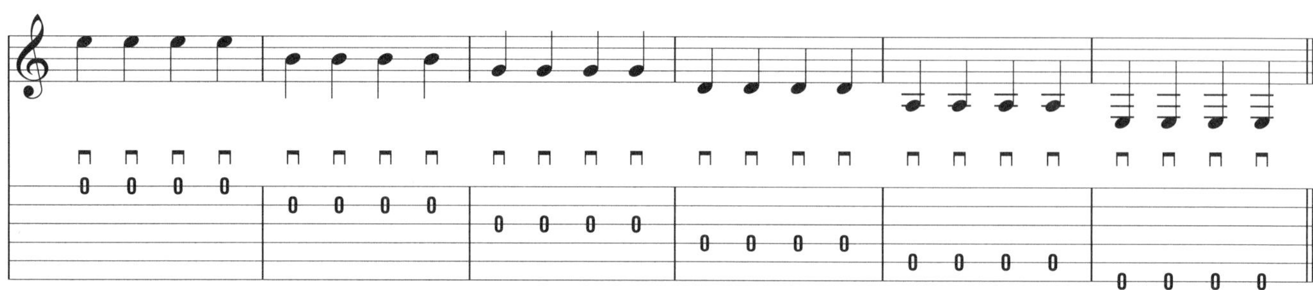

In this exercise, we'll use down and up strokes, but be sure to make every down stroke a rest stroke.

FIG. 17

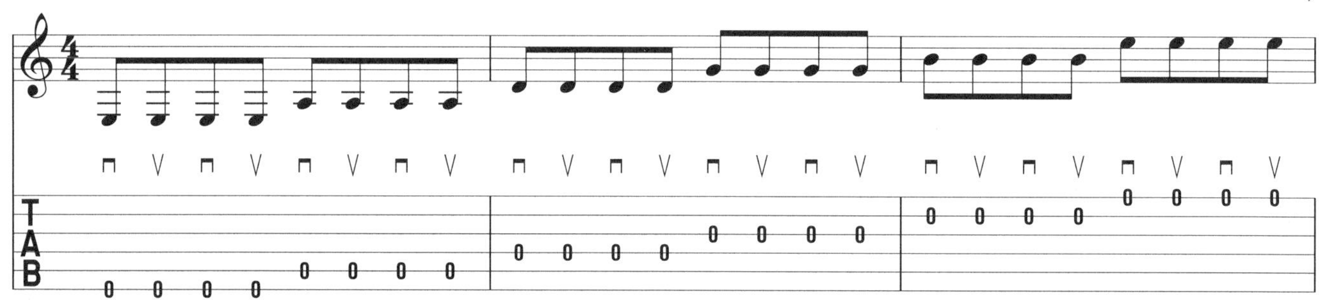

Picking Rules

There are some very specific rules regarding picking technique:

1. Every down stroke is a rest stroke.
2. Always start with a down stroke when switching strings.
3. Always finish a phrase with a down stroke.

It's important to remark that not everyone adheres strictly to these rules, but watch any accomplished player and you'll notice that they mostly use down strokes, especially on slow and medium tempos. The following exercises will help you develop your picking technique. You should use them as warm-up exercises that you play every day with a metronome. They use only open strings which will allow you to focus solely on your right hand. Start slowly and gradually increase the tempo. Be patient and always make sure you are not forcing the speed and playing with tension.

Triplets are used extensively in the style and are one of the most important things to practice since they often require double-down strokes. (If we play three notes per string and then switch to a new string we start with a down stroke, meaning two consecutive down strokes.) We'll start by playing triplets on a single string.

FIG. 18

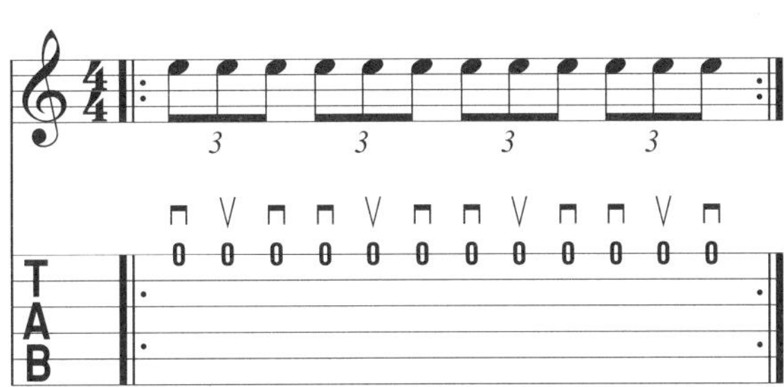

Now, we'll cover all six strings. Remember to use the rest stroke!

FIG. 19

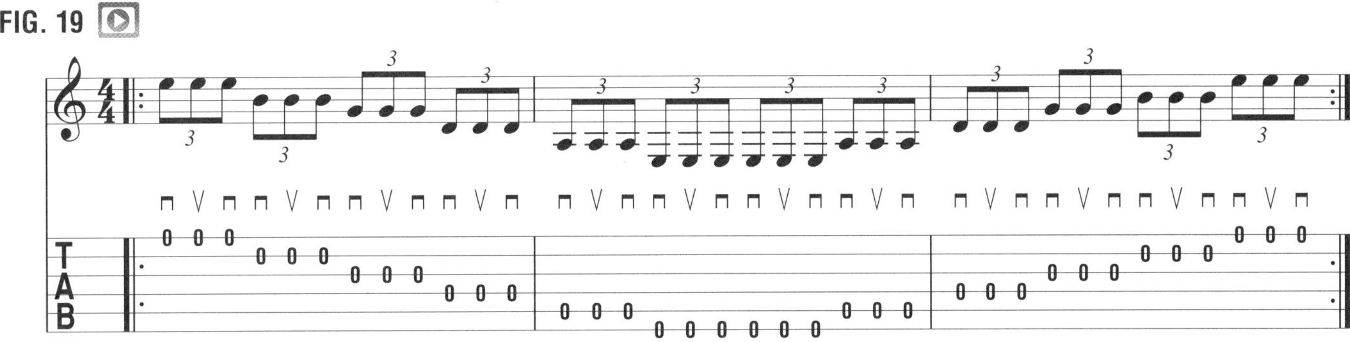

Now, we'll work on the elbow fulcrum movement by skipping strings.

FIG. 20

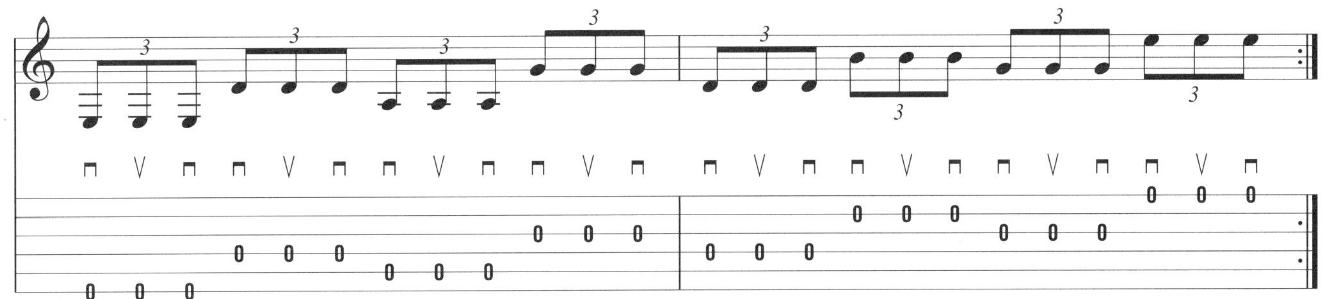

Consider these exercises as a starting point. Once you've understood the concepts of the rest stroke and the picking system, it's fairly easy to come up with your own. It's also possible to multi-task. When you learn a new lick, scale, or arpeggio, start by practicing it slowly, using just down strokes, then apply the picking rules.

Navigating the Fretboard

Fingerings

Before we move on, we need to say a word about fingerings. Most players use all four fingers, some use just three (leaving out the pinky), and a rare few adamantly imitate Django's two-finger technique. This makes fingerings a difficult thing to codify. What we can say is that the style involves a great deal of horizontal playing. In the following examples, we will compare a typical fingering with a Gypsy-style fingering.

Typical Fingering

FIG. 21

Gypsy-Style Fingering

Notice the shift in position that occurs from the third to fourth notes in measure 1 and from the fourth to fifth notes in measure 2.

FIG. 22

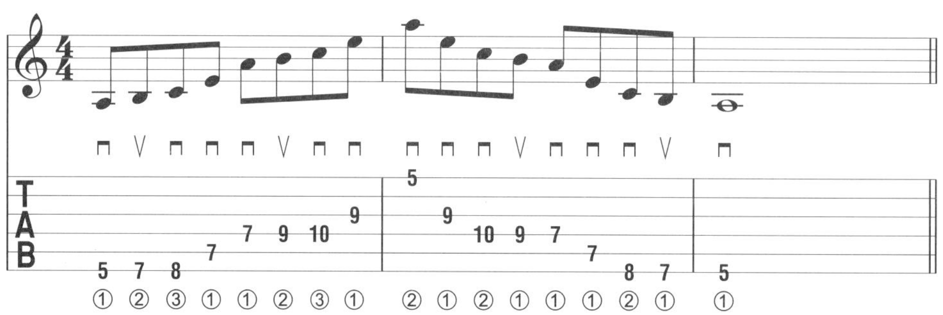

Typical Fingering

FIG. 23

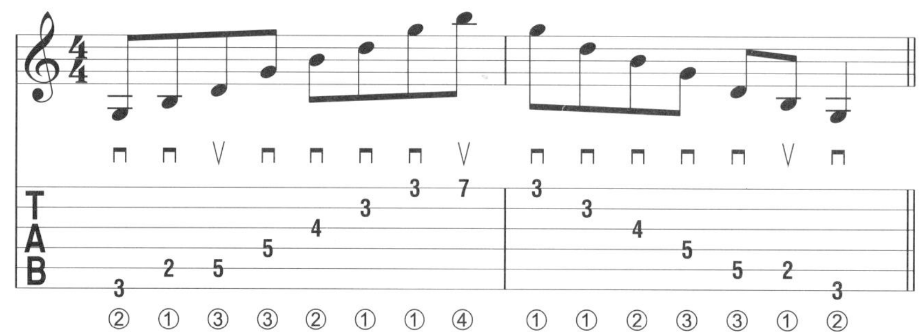

Gypsy-Style Fingering

In this example, we use only two fingers. In some cases, this can actually be a quicker and cleaner way to execute a phrase. That doesn't mean you should force yourself to copy the master. Experiment with different fingerings in the examples that follow. Find what works best for you, but be aware that horizontal shifts can be just as fast as a vertical approach.

FIG. 24

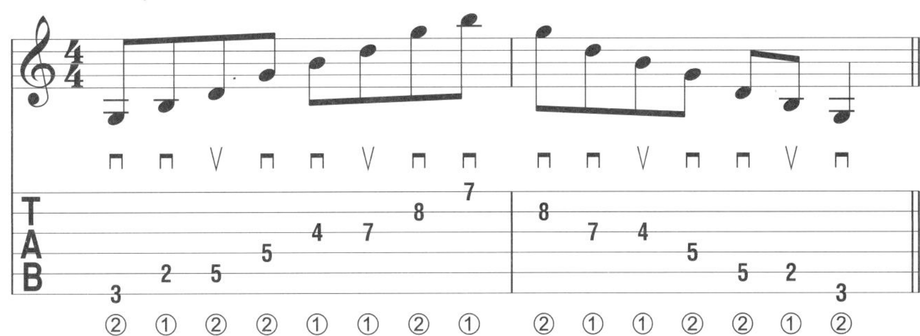

CHAPTER 4

SOLOING WITH ARPEGGIOS

Arpeggios are basically the stuff that a Gypsy jazz solo is made of. Any improvisation is based on weaving chord tones together, either using a scale or chromatic movements. You can't do that without knowing where those tones are, i.e., the arpeggio. In this section, we are going to study the must-know arpeggios in the Gypsy jazz style: minor, major, dominant, and diminished.

Most guitarists, whatever the style, see arpeggios as they relate to a chord form, which is how we'll proceed here. In these diagrams, the fretboard is divided into four basic major and minor shapes, each built around a chord form. These chord forms are moveable but based on common open chord shapes. Sometimes, the arpeggios work neatly within the shapes. Other times, they navigate between two or more. Think of these shapes as the basic structures on which the arpeggio patterns are based. Note: the numbers that appear in each diagram correspond to scale degrees, not fingerings!

Major Arpeggio Shapes

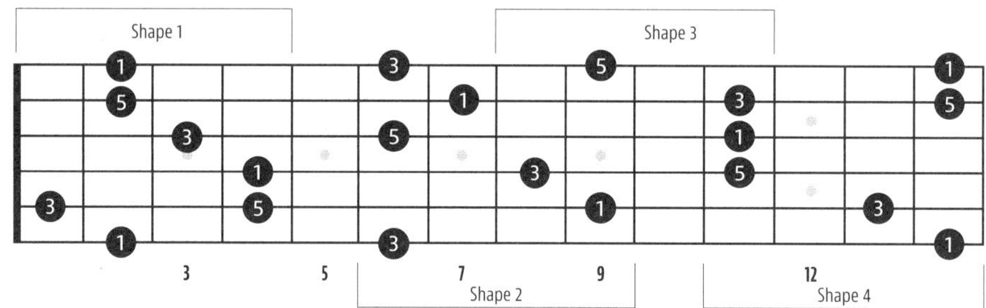

Shape 1 = E Major Form

Shape 2 = C Major Form

Shape 3 = A Major Form

Shape 4 = G Major Form

Minor Arpeggio Shapes

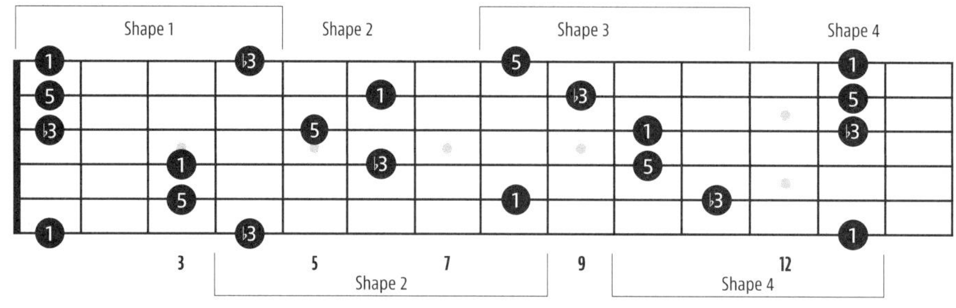

Shape 1 = E Minor Form

Shape 2 = C Minor Form

Shape 3 = A Minor Form

Shape 4 = G Minor Form

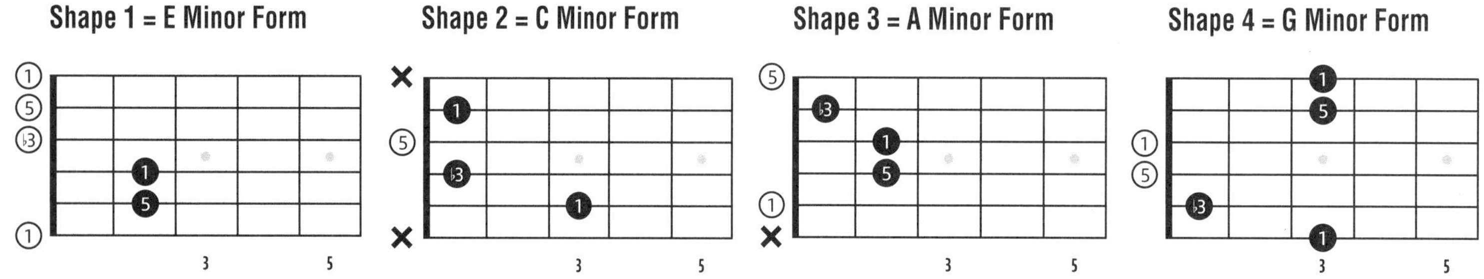

Exploring Major and Minor Arpeggios

In the following examples, we'll play over a chord progression similar to the A section of "Minor Swing." We'll start simply, running up one arpeggio and down another. This might not sound particularly musical at first, but it is important that you become familiar with these basic shapes. As we progress, you'll learn increasingly complex phrases and we'll add tones to enhance the arpeggios. (The diagrams indicate the tones being used in each phrase. Tones that belong to the shape but aren't used appear in white.)

- Measures 1 and 2: Am arpeggio using shape 1.
- Measures 3 and 4: Dm arpeggio using shape 3.
- Measures 5 and 6: E arpeggio using shape 2.
- Measures 7 and 8: Am arpeggio using shape 1.

FIG. 25

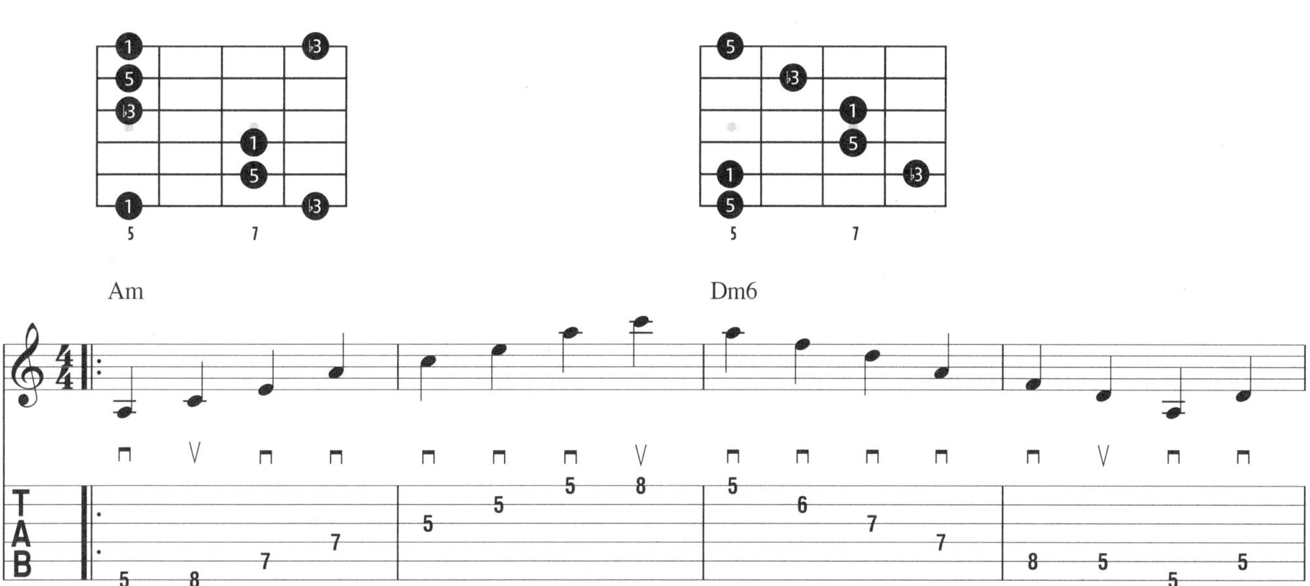

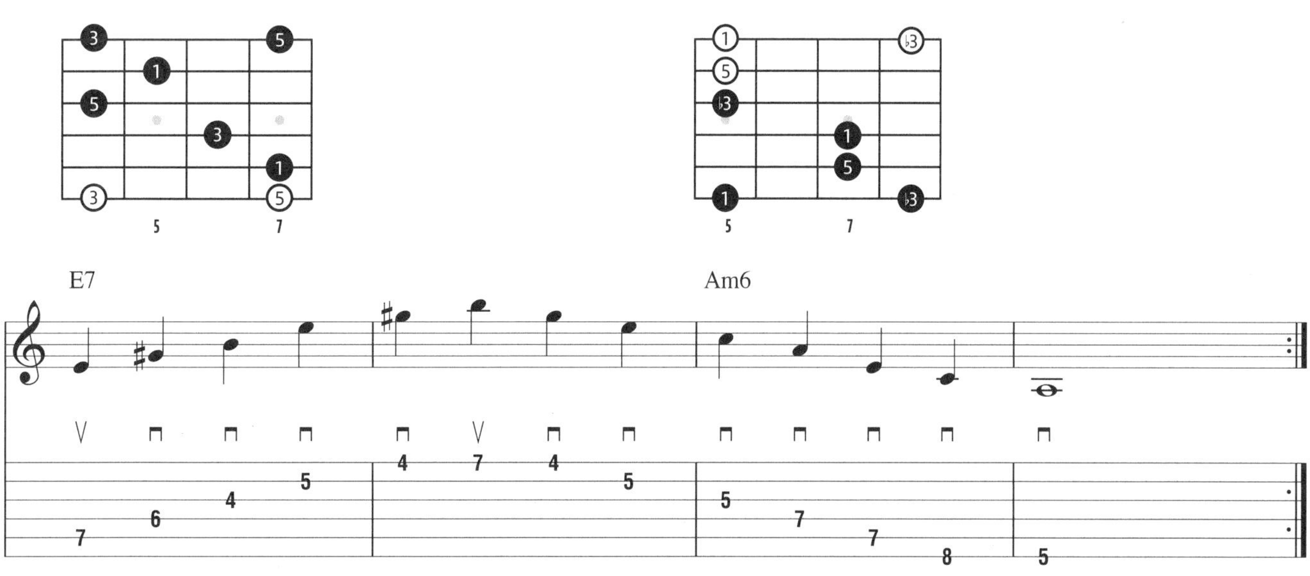

- Measures 1 and 2: We start our Am arpeggio in shape 1 but quickly shift into shape 2. This would be a much more common path in the style.
- Measures 3 and 4: Dm arpeggio using shape 1.
- Measures 5 and 6: E arpeggio using shape 4.
- Measures 7 and 8: Am arpeggio using shape 2 and finishing in shape 1. Note that the final note in this example is an E, which is the 5th of the Am chord. Phrases don't absolutely need to finish on the root. Any note in the triad will give a phrase a sense of resolution.

FIG. 26

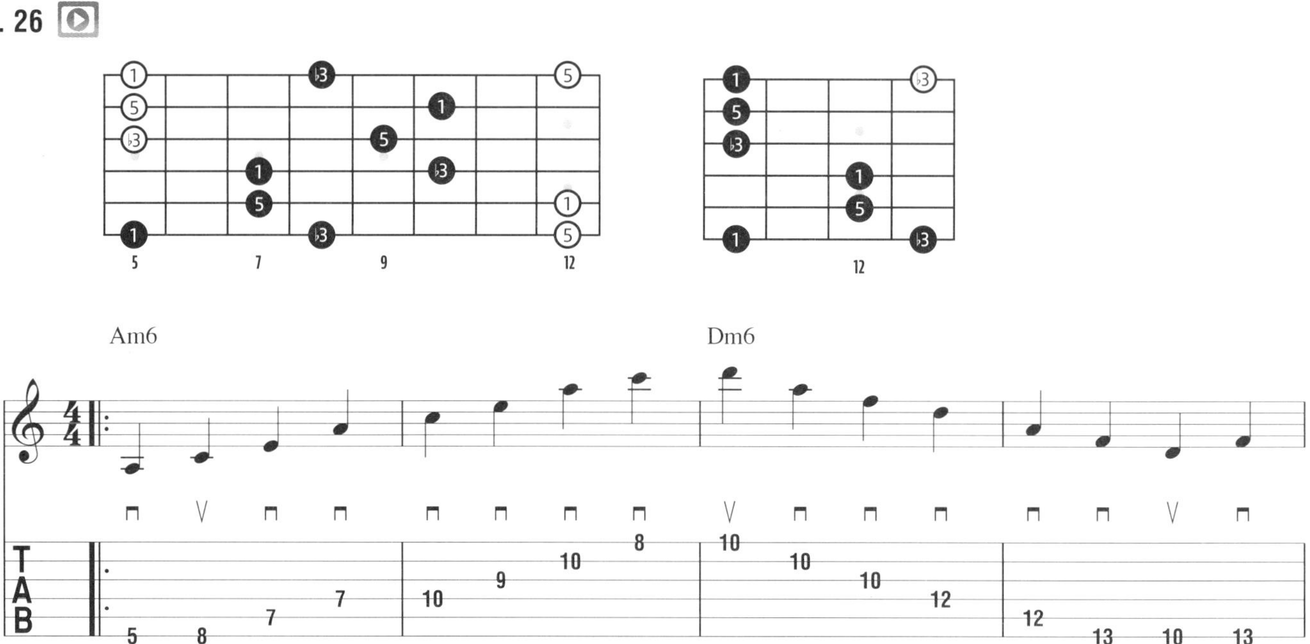

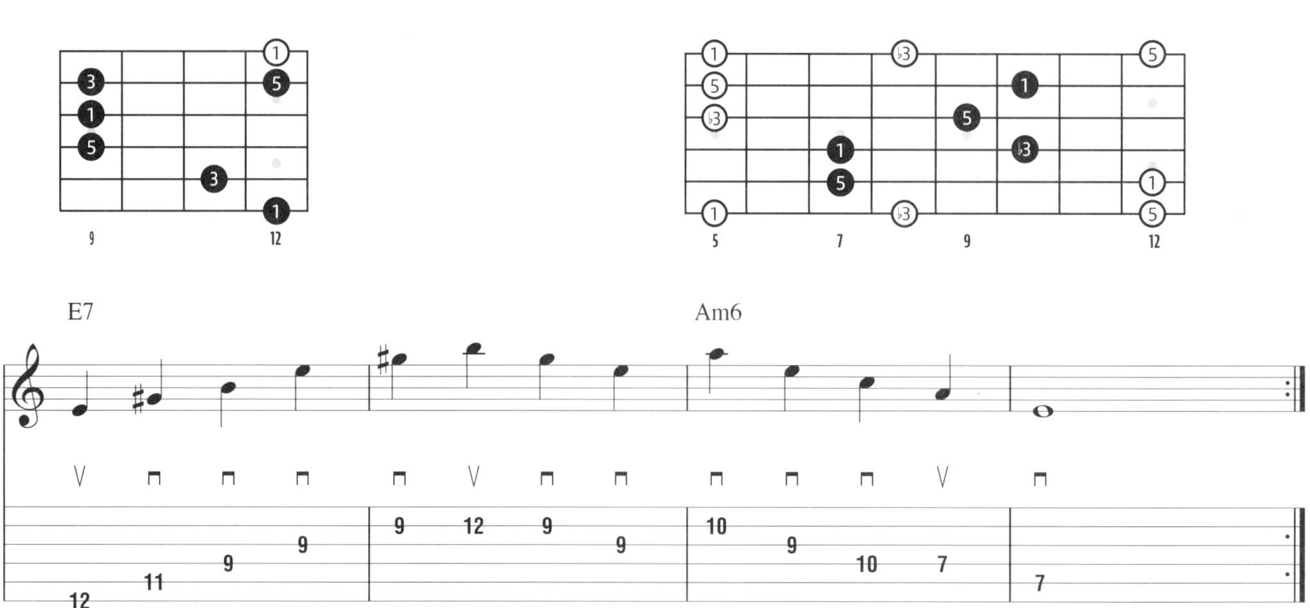

Adding Notes and Dominant Arpeggios

Adding the 2nd

It's common in the style to add the 2nd and/or 6th degree of the Aeolian mode to a minor arpeggio. This creates a kind of arpeggio/scale hybrid that is very effective. Just adding one of these tones makes the arpeggio sound much more musical. We'll start by adding the 2nd (B) over Am and E over Dm. To the E arpeggio, we'll now add the ♭7th (D), making it an E7.

- Measures 1 and 2: Am arpeggio shifting from shape 1 to shape 2.
- Measures 3 and 4: Dm arpeggio descending from shape 4 to shape 3.
- Measures 5 and 6: E7 arpeggio using shape 3.
- Measures 7 and 8: Am arpeggio using shape 1.

FIG. 27

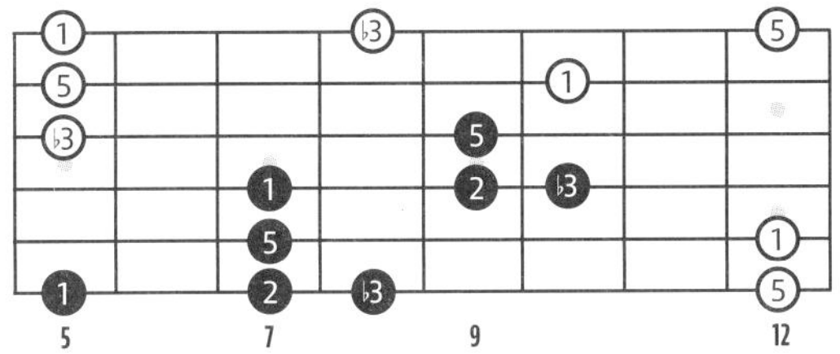

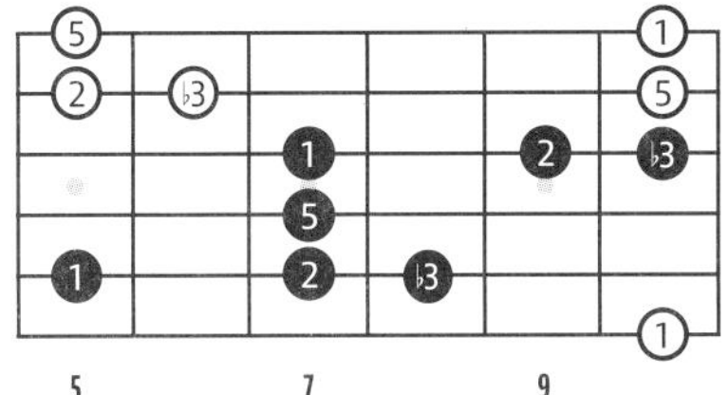

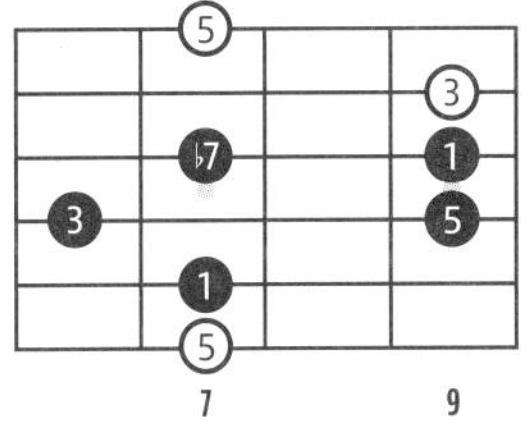

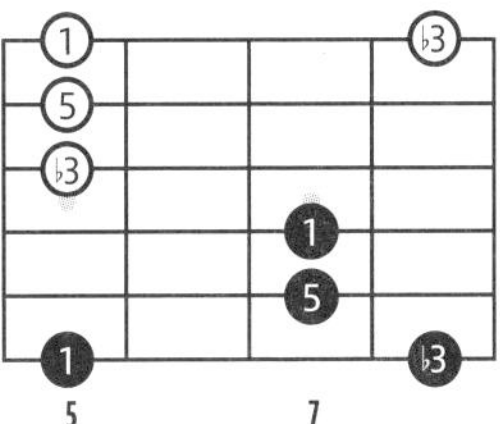

- Measures 1 and 2: Am arpeggio using shape 1.
- Measures 3 and 4: Dm arpeggio using shape 3.
- Measures 5 and 6: E7 arpeggio starting in shape 2 and finishing in shape 3.
- Measures 7 and 8: Am arpeggio descending shape 2 with the last note in shape 1.

FIG. 28

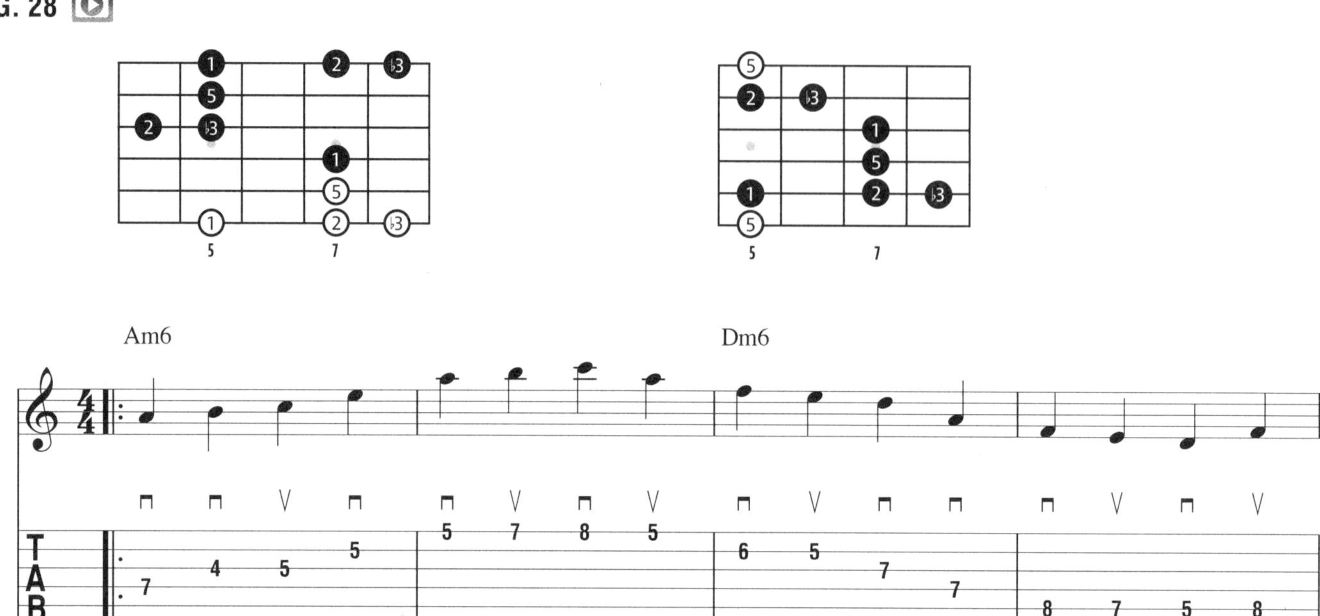

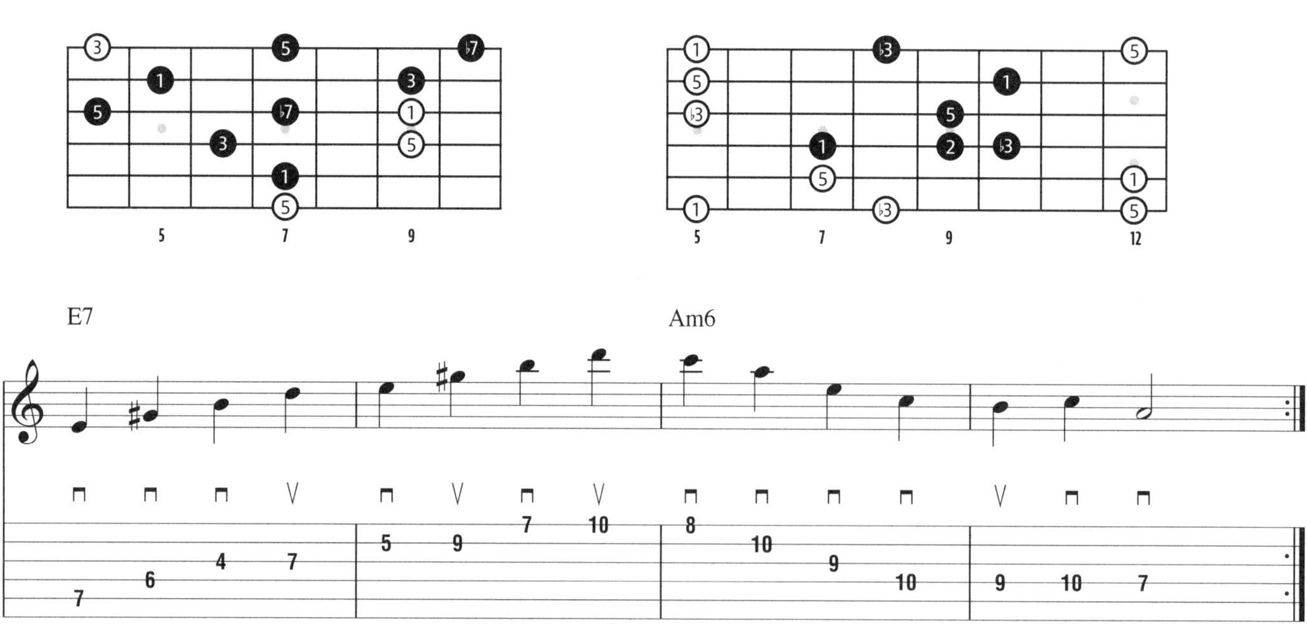

Adding the 6th

The tone that really gives a minor arpeggio that Gypsy sound is the 6th. We'll add that now to the Am and Dm arpeggios.

- Measures 1 and 2: Am arpeggio starting in shape 1 and shifting to shape 2.
- Measures 3 and 4: Dm arpeggio using shape 1.
- Measures 5 and 6: E7 arpeggio using shape 4.
- Measures 7 and 8: Am arpeggio shifting from shape 2 to shape 1.

FIG. 29

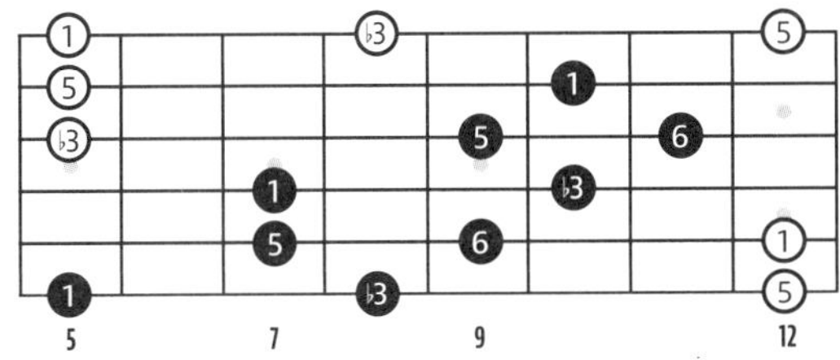

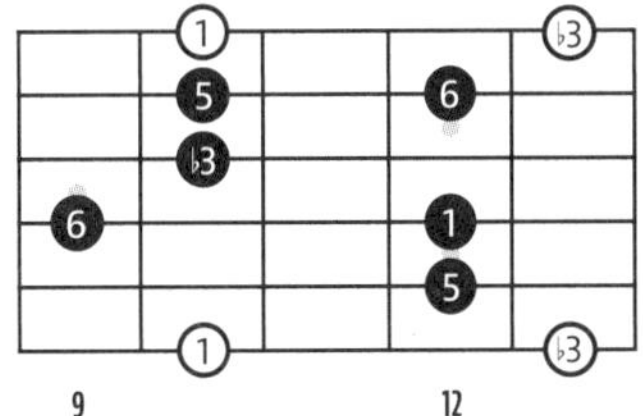

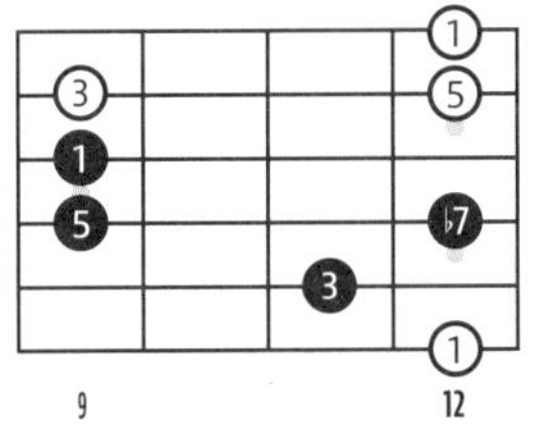

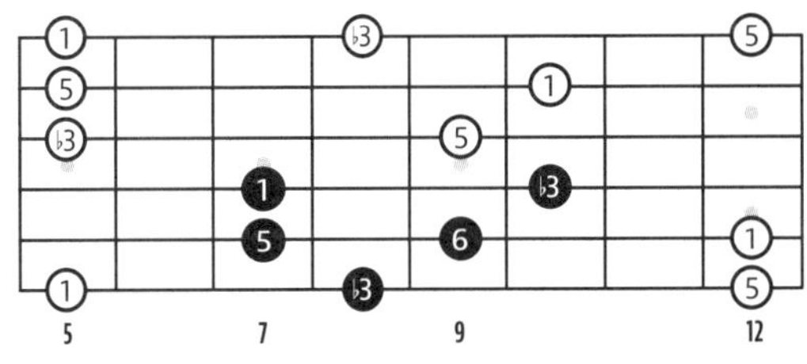

- Measures 1 and 2: One of my favorite minor 6 runs, starting in shape 3, running down shape 2, and finishing on the root in shape 1.
- Measures 3 and 4: Dm arpeggio using shape 4.
- Measures 5 and 6: E7 arpeggio using shape 3.
- Measures 7 and 8: Am arpeggio starting in shape 2 and finishing in shape 1.

FIG. 30

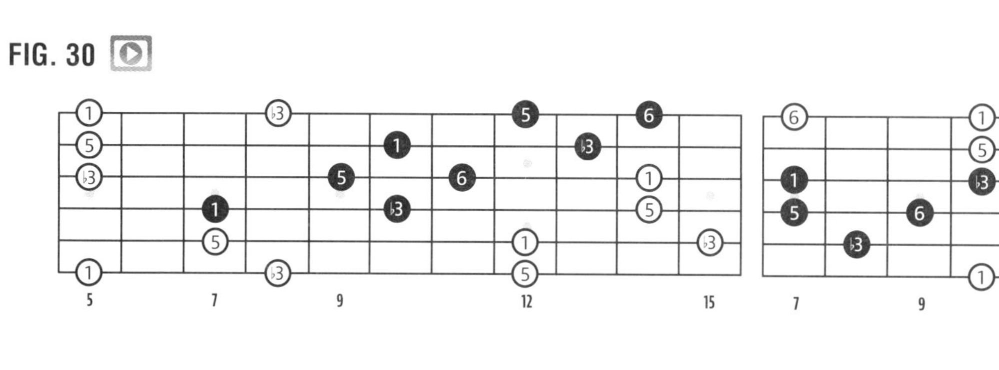

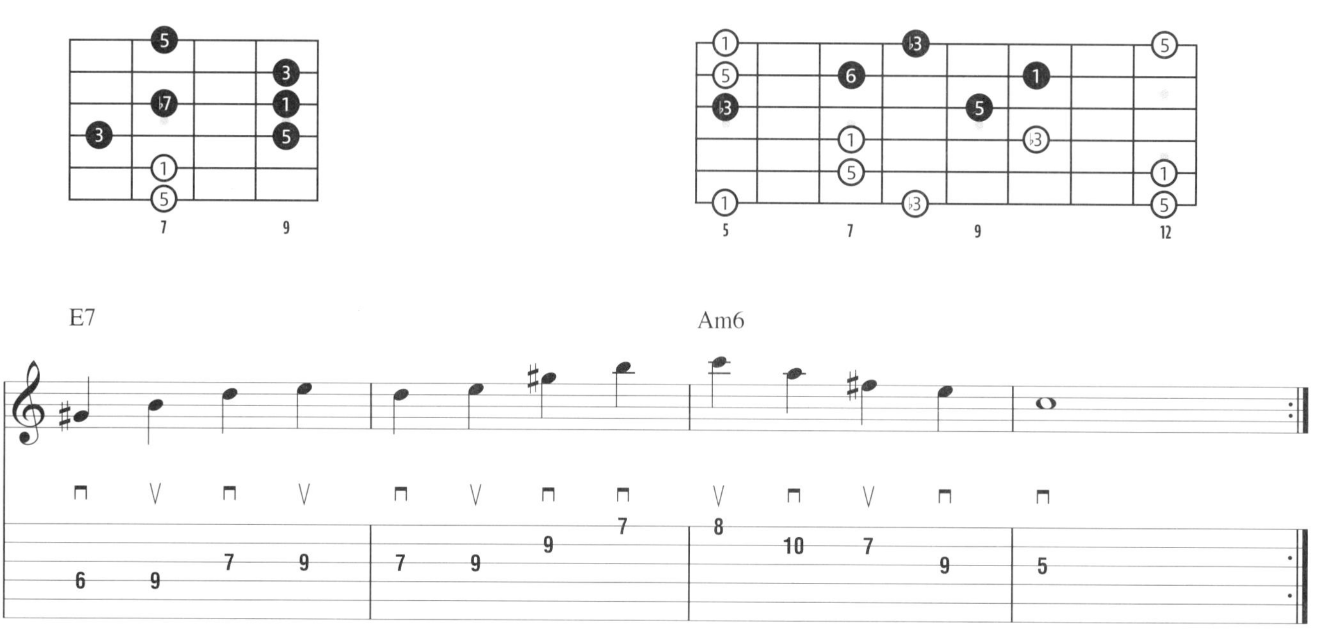

Dominant 7♭9 Arpeggios

Another signature sound in Gypsy jazz is the use of the ♭9 on a dominant chord. This merits some explanation, as knowing when to use it can be tricky. A dominant 7♭9 is an altered chord. In jazz usage, a dominant 7th chord is considered altered if either or both the 5th and 9th are raised or lowered. C7♭9, C7♯9, C7♭5, C7♯5, C7♯5♭9, and C7♯5♯9 are all examples of altered chords. Altered chords can be used when the following chord is a 4th above:

- D7 chord followed by a Gm chord could be altered.
- A7 followed by a D chord could be altered.
- C7 followed by an F7 chord could be altered.

In the following examples, we have an E7 moving to an A minor. Since that is the movement of a 4th, the E7 can be altered, so we will add the ♭9. There are, of course, other possible alterations, but since the ♭9 is the most common in Gypsy jazz, it will be our main focus.

The first example is built around shape 2.

FIG. 31

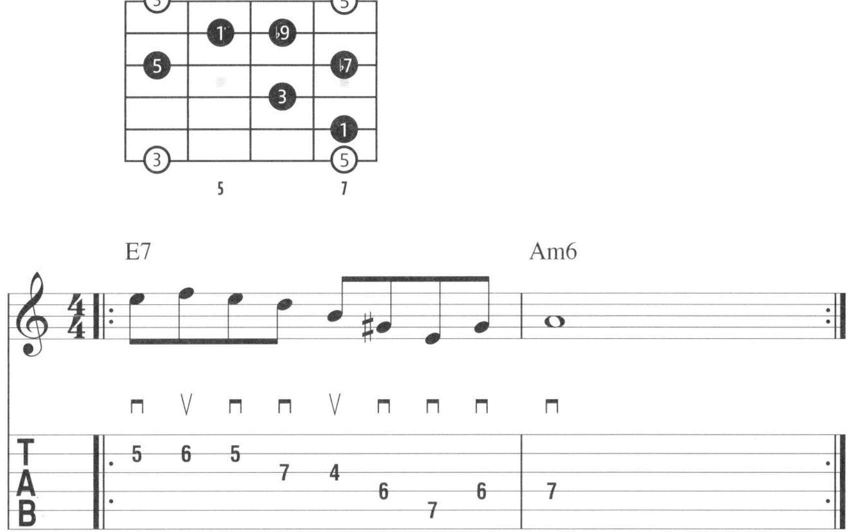

The second example is built around shape 3.

FIG. 32

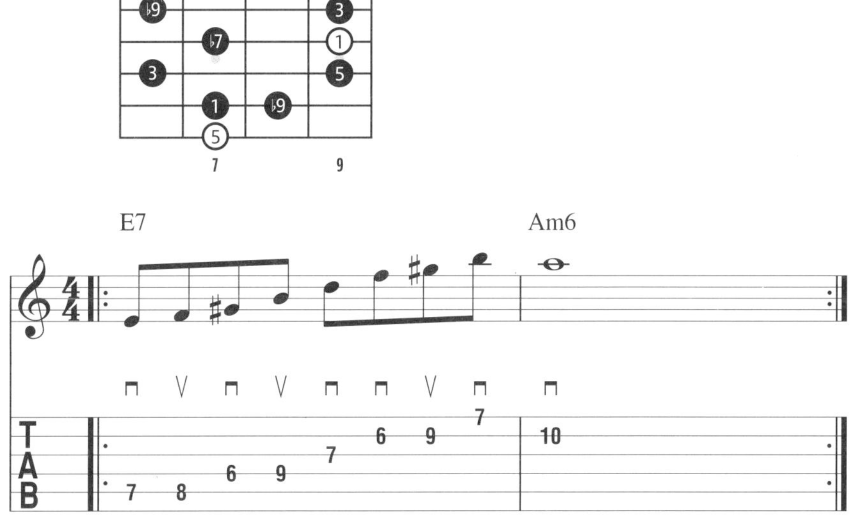

The third example is built around shape 4.

FIG. 33

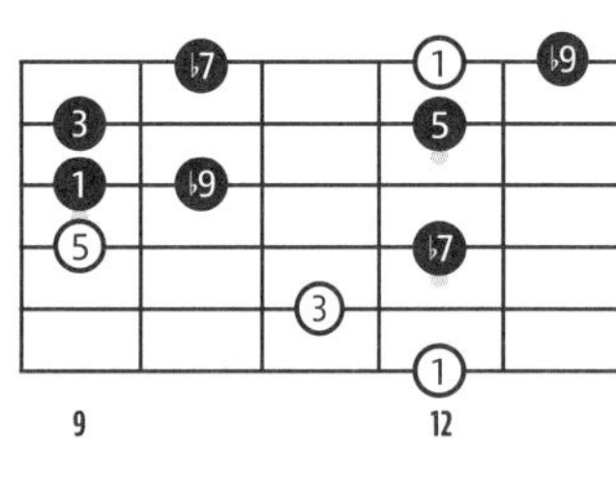

The fourth example is built around shape 1.

FIG. 34

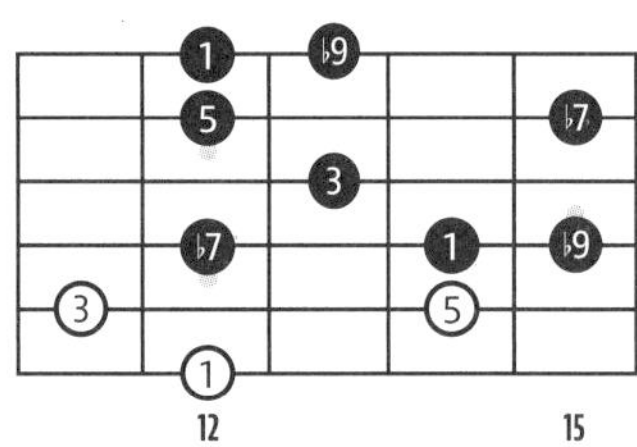

The Diminished Arpeggio

In short, the diminished arpeggio is another way to play a dominant 7♭9 arpeggio. Again, some explanation is necessary.

What Is a Diminished 7th Chord?

A diminished 7th chord contains a root, ♭3rd, ♭5th, and ♭♭7th (the ♭♭7 is the same note as the 6th). These tones are all a minor 3rd (three half steps) from each other, creating a symmetrical pattern on the fretboard. This symmetry makes them rather unique because the same shape can be moved up or down the fretboard in three-fret increments without changing the chord. Only the order of the notes changes, resulting in only three different diminished chords/scales.

How Are Diminished 7th Chords Used?

Diminished 7th chords are often used as passing chords, but by far their most common usage is as a voicing for a dominant 7♭9 chord. Let's compare an E7♭9 with a F°7 chord:

- E7♭9 = E–G♯–B–D–F
- F°7 = F–A♭–B–D

As you can see, the only note missing from the F°7 chord is the E (A♭ and G♯ are the same note). This makes it a perfect voicing for an E7♭9 chord.

In the following examples, we'll use an F°7 arpeggio over an E7 chord that resolves to Am. You'll notice how the symmetry of the diminished arpeggio gives the fingerings a distinctive, stair-like pattern. Since we are using this F°7 arpeggio over an E7♭9 chord, the notes in the diagram show the E7♭9 arpeggio.

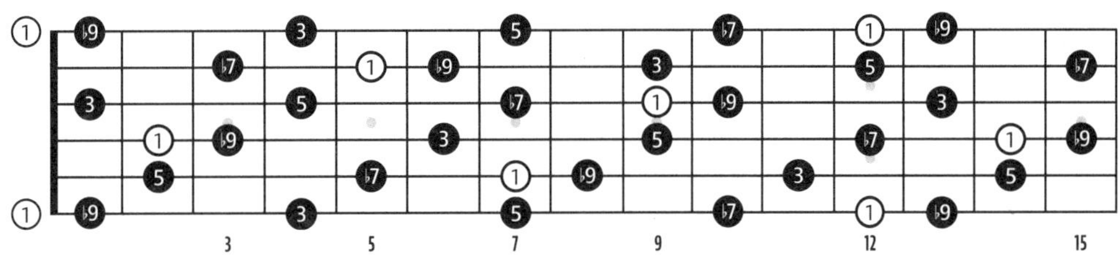

FIG. 35

FIG. 36

FIG. 37

In this last example, we see how a diminished chord can be moved in three-fret increments, all inversions of E7♭9.

FIG. 38

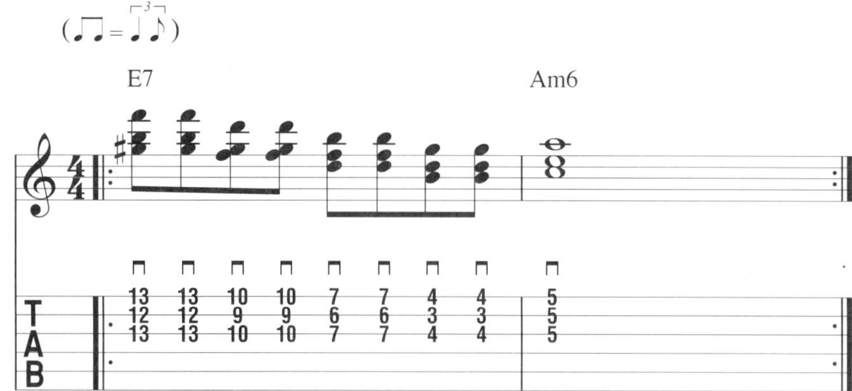

Now, we'll take all the arpeggios we've studied so far to create a solo over a progression similar to "Minor Swing." Make sure you understand how each tone relates to the chord it's played over.

FIG. 39 

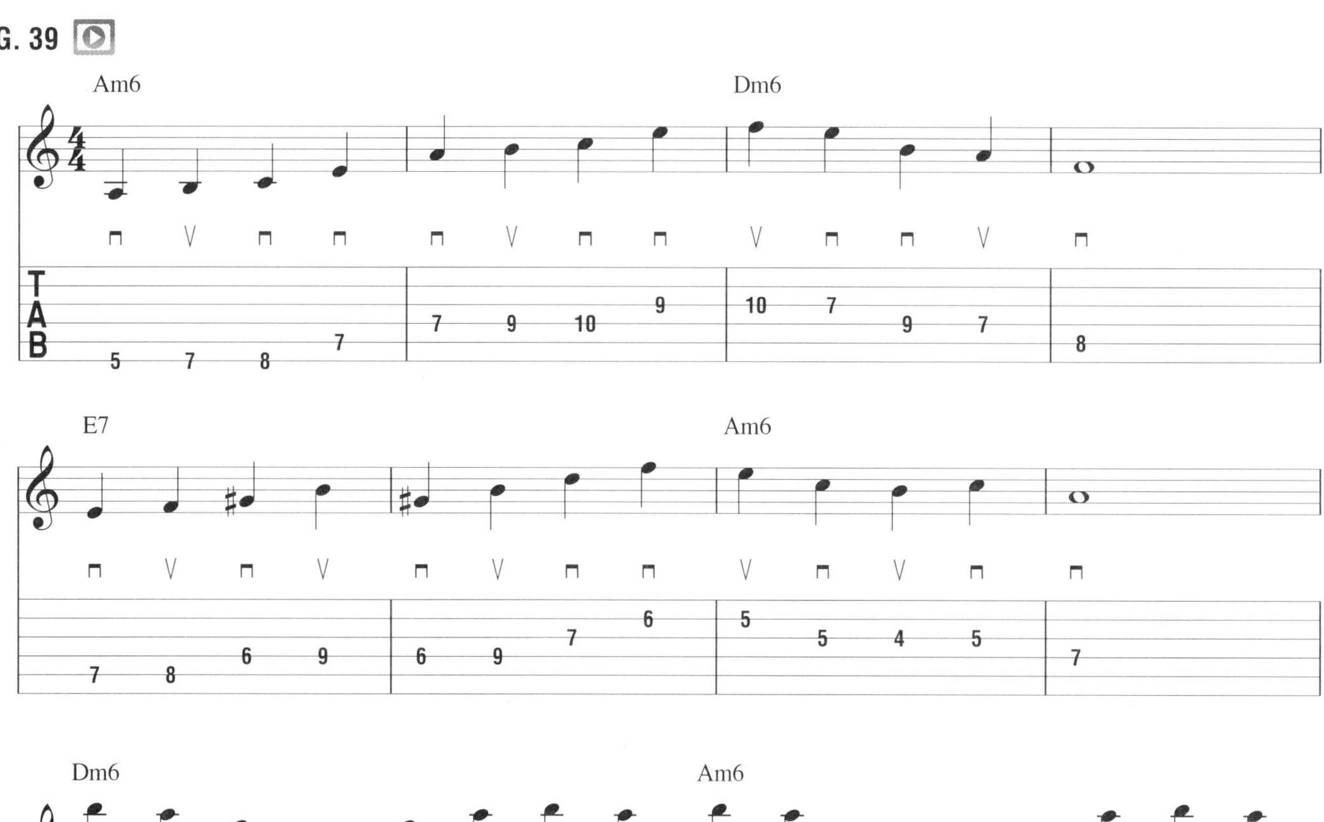

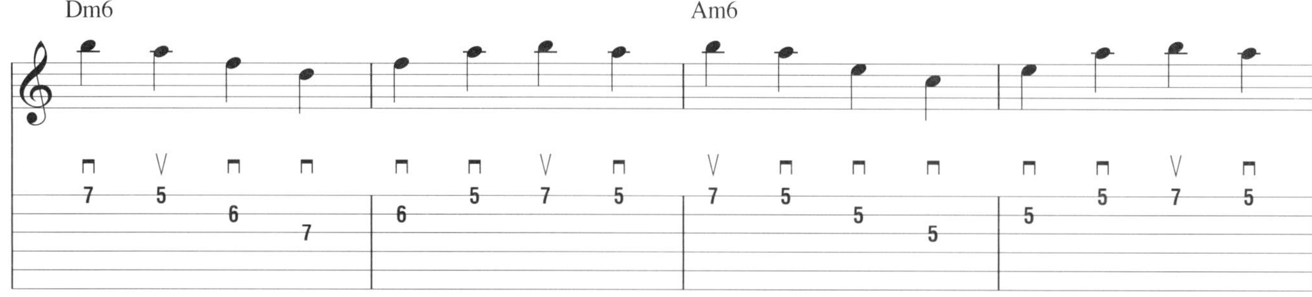

Major 7 Arpeggios

In the next section, we'll shift our focus from minor to major arpeggios. In the Gypsy style, players often use major 7th arpeggios, or major scale/arpeggio hybrids by adding the 6th and 7th to the basic triad. Note that any major arpeggio can be played over any major chord type. You can play a Dmaj7 arpeggio over a D6 chord and vice-versa. We'll also enhance our dominant arpeggio by adding the 9th. As a general rule, the 9th can be added to a dominant chord when playing in a major key. To provide context, we'll use a chord progression similar to "Lulu Swing," a Gypsy jazz standard.

- Measures 1 and 2: Dmaj7 arpeggio using shape 3.
- Measures 3 and 4: E7 arpeggio using shape 2.
- Measures 5 and 6: A9 arpeggio using shape 1.
- Measures 7 and 8: Dmaj7 arpeggio using shapes 4 and 3.

FIG. 40 

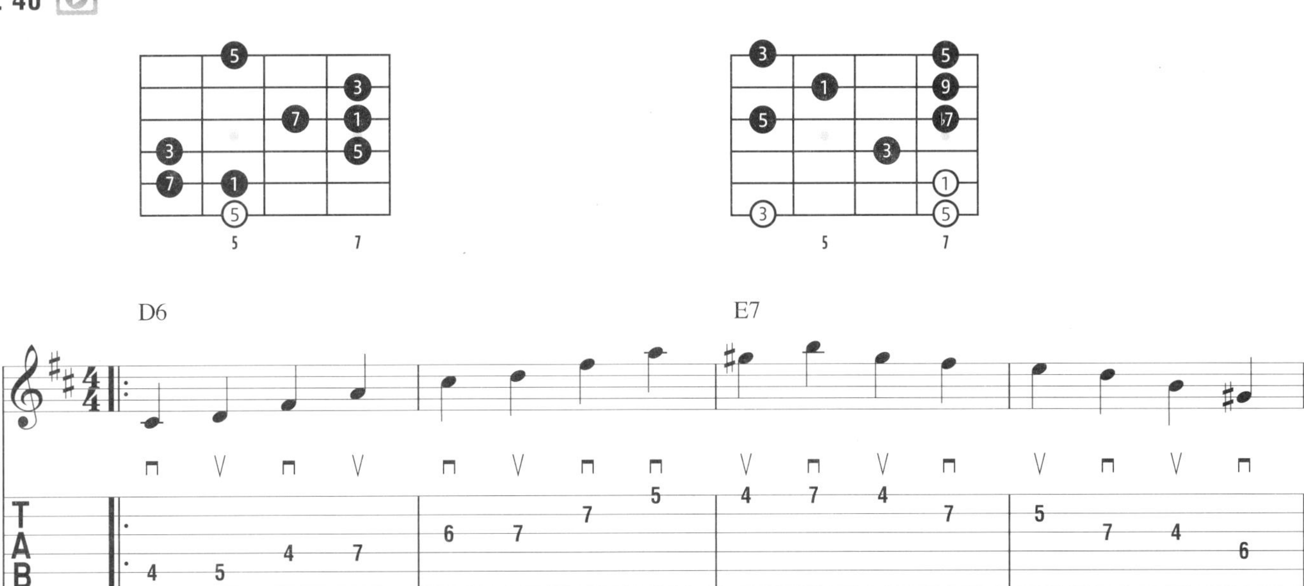

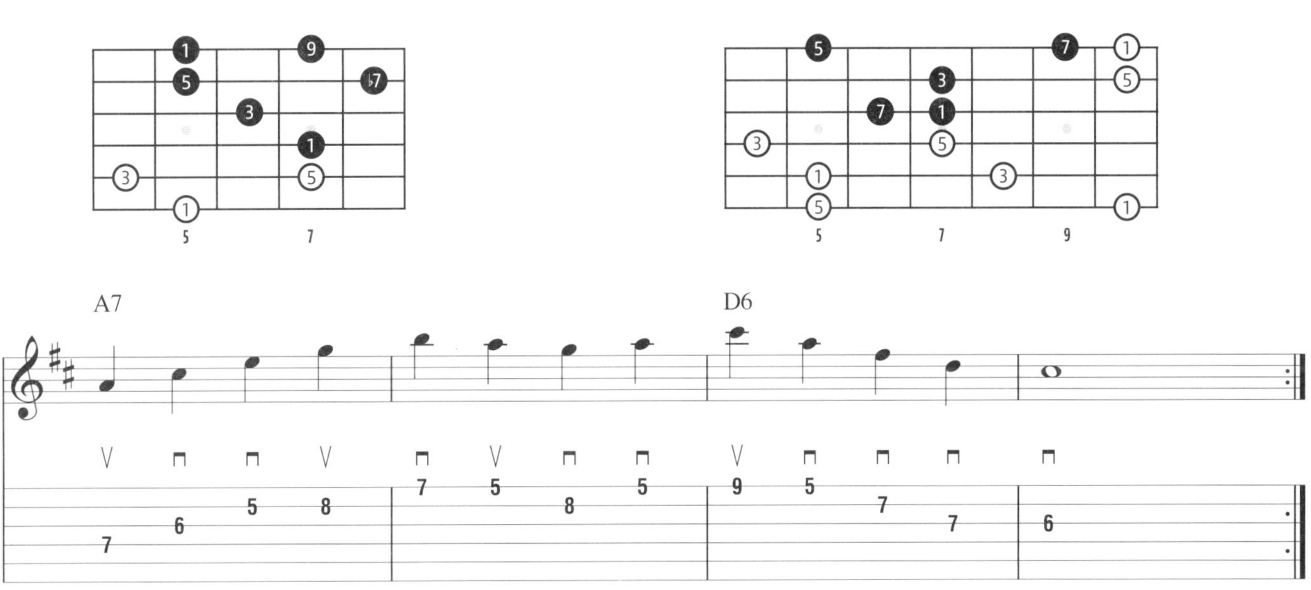

- Measures 1 and 2: D hybrid major scale/arpeggio lick.
- Measures 3 and 4: E9 arpeggio lick using shape 4.
- Measures 5 and 6: A9 arpeggio using shape 3.
- Measures 7 and 8: a D6 arpeggio lick using shapes 1 and 2.

FIG. 41 

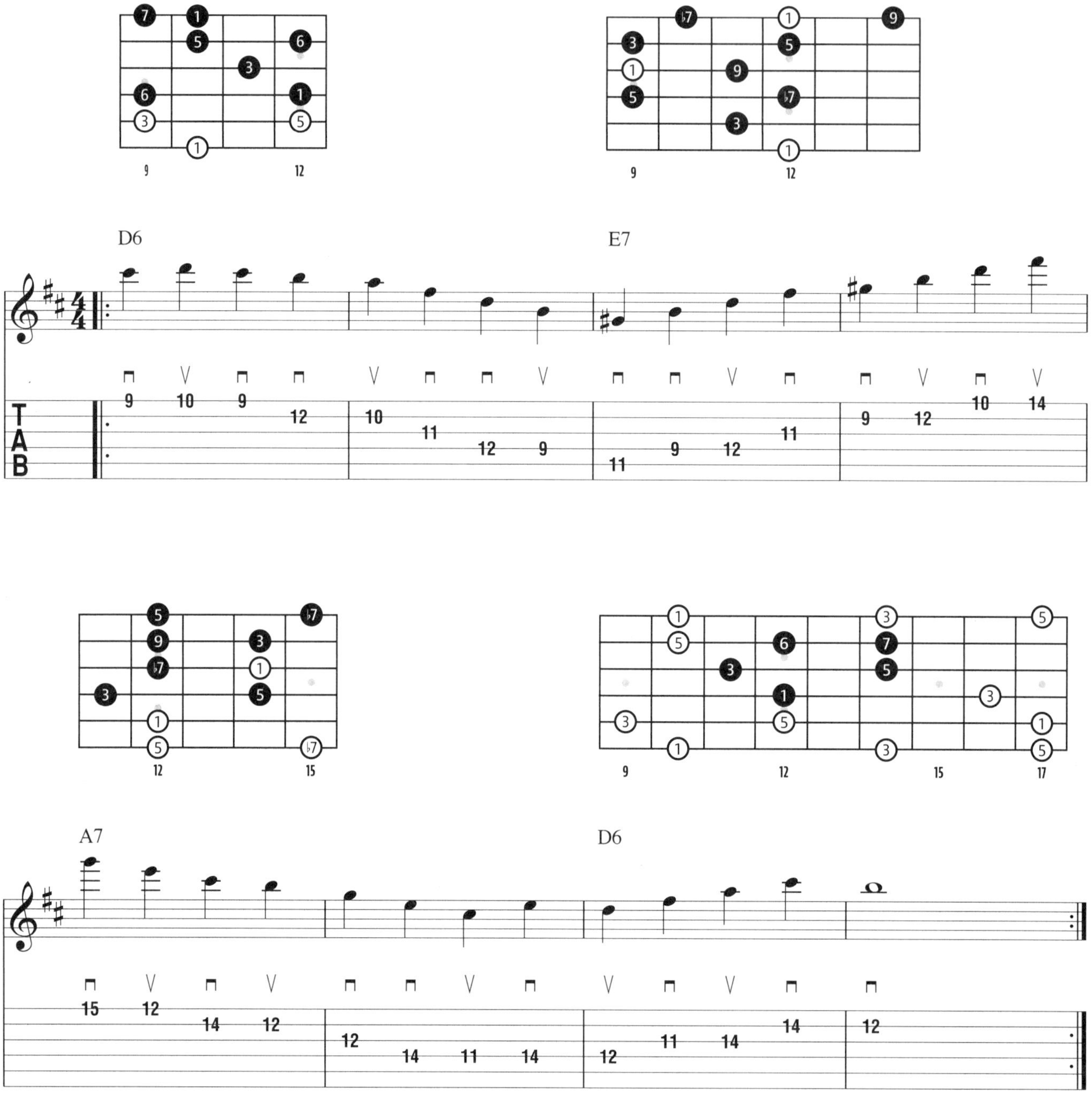

D6 E7

A7 D6

We'll now use these ideas to create a solo over a progression similar to "Django's Castle." For this solo, we'll make the leap to eighth-note phrases. Make sure you understand how each tone relates to the chord it is played over.

FIG. 42

These arpeggio studies should give you the foundation you need to understand and assimilate the techniques we are going to learn in the next part of the book. Apply the following rules and you'll start to feel it come together:

- Always know what tone you are on in relation to the chord.
- Always use the proper picking technique.
- Always play tension free, aiming for precision, not speed.

In the next section, we'll explore some soloing techniques commonly used in the Gypsy jazz style. We'll use common chord progressions to provide context, keeping the phrases to eighth-note figures to facilitate the learning process.

CHAPTER 5

SOLOING WITH NEIGHBORING TONES AND ENCLOSURES

Neighboring Tones

Using *neighboring tones* is an easy way to spice up an arpeggio, and it's a device that Gypsy jazz players use a lot. It's as simple as this: before you play a chord tone, play the note one fret below it.

The diagram shows tones used in each phrase. Chord tones are circles, neighboring tones are squares.

This example is in C based on shape 1.

FIG. 43

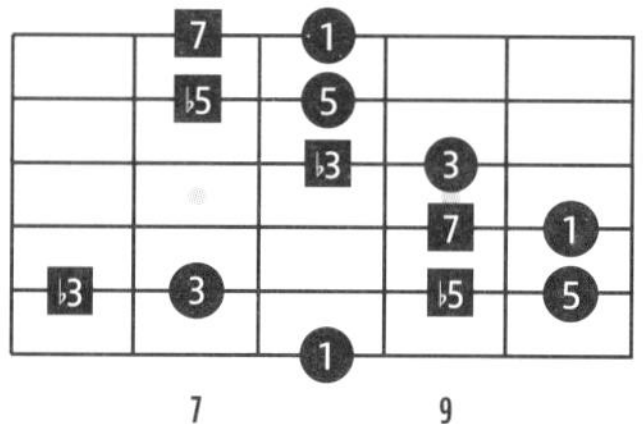

This example is in F based on shape 3.

FIG. 44

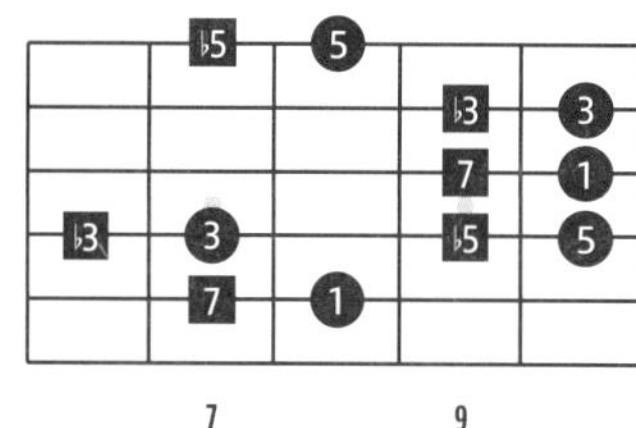

This example is in Am based on shape 1.

FIG. 45

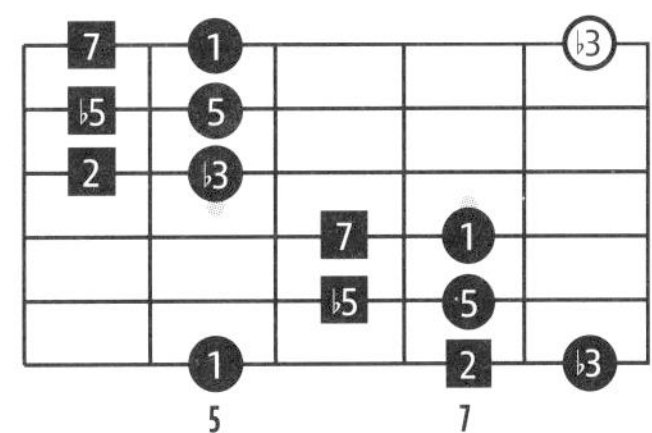

This example is in Dm based on shape 3.

FIG. 46

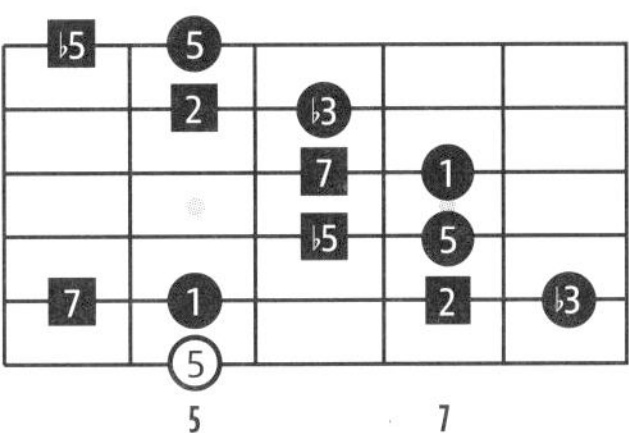

Enclosures

An *enclosure* is a three-note phrase that circles a chord tone. It starts on the neighboring note below, then jumps to the scale note above, finishing on the chord tone itself.

The following example is over a C chord (shape 1), so the upper note of the enclosure is from the C major scale.

FIG. 47 

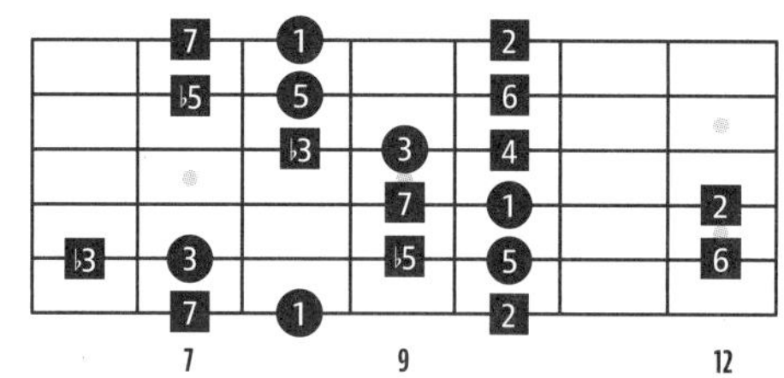

This example is over an F chord (chord shape 3), so the upper note of the enclosure is from the F major scale.

FIG. 48

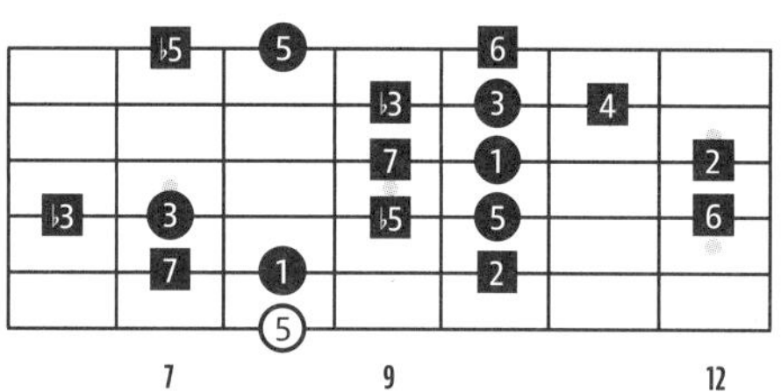

This example is over an Am chord (chord shape 1), so the note above is from the A minor scale.

FIG. 49

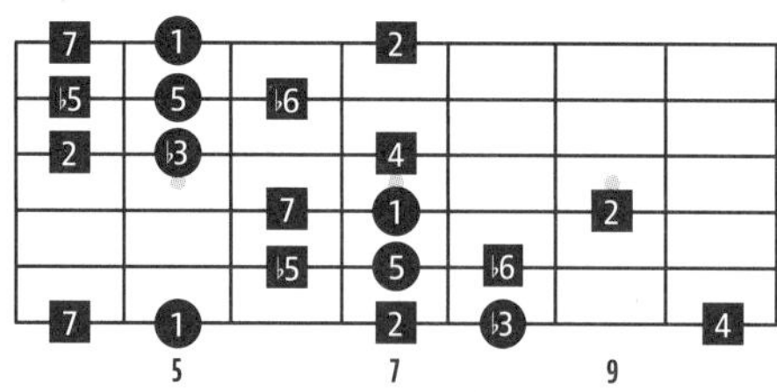

This example is over a Dm chord (chord shape 3) so the note above is from the D minor scale.

FIG. 50

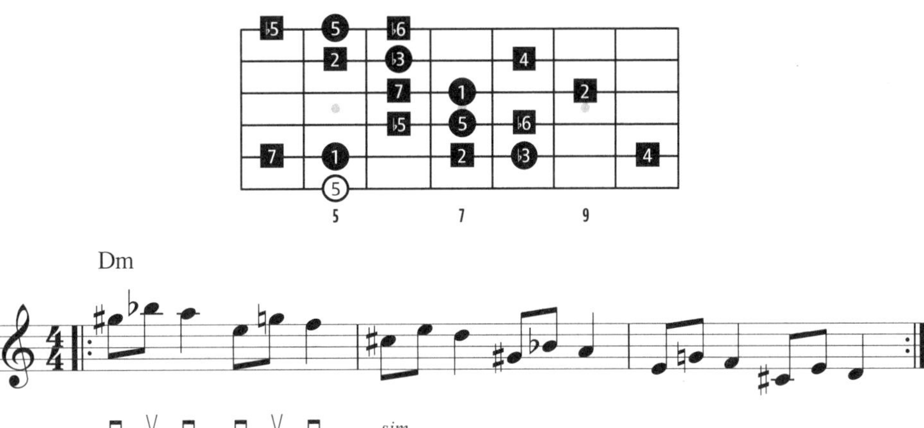

This is one of Django's signature major chord licks based on the enclosure concept.

FIG. 51

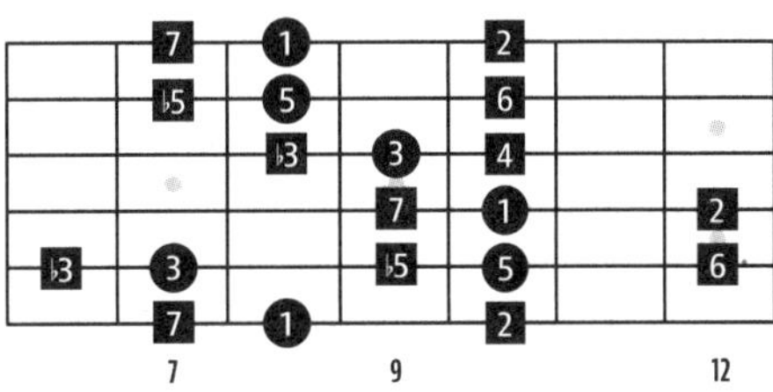

Common Enclosures

Here is one more enclosure lick that I've heard practically every player use. It can be used over a number of different chord types. On the next page, we have three variations over an Am6 chord.

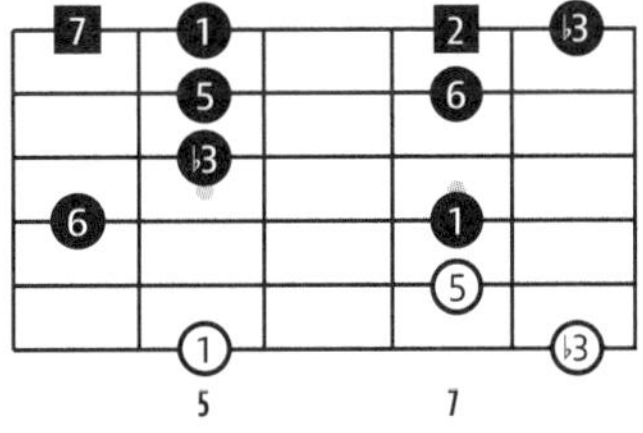

FIG. 52

FIG. 53

FIG. 54

Now, we'll put all these ideas into context by using them in a solo. The chord progression is similar to the A section of "After You've Gone," a standard in the Gypsy jazz repertoire. The solo is almost entirely comprised of arpeggios, using neighboring tones and enclosures. Take special note of the enclosure licks used in measure 3 (over the Cm6 chord) and in measure 11 (over the D7 chord). This is essentially the same phrase but used over two different chord types. Be sure to analyze how the tones line up relative to each chord. The last enclosure, over the G6 chord, is fairly straightforward, but the rhythm shifts so that the neighboring tones fall on strong beats creating added tension.

FIG. 55

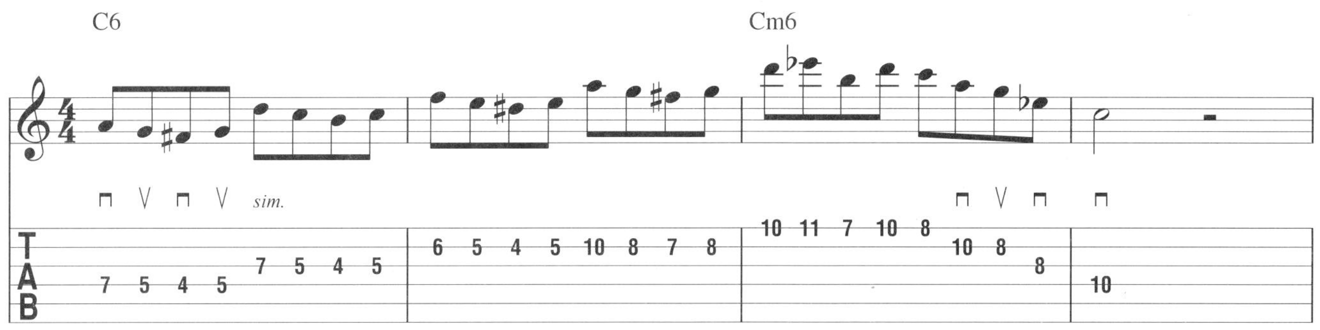

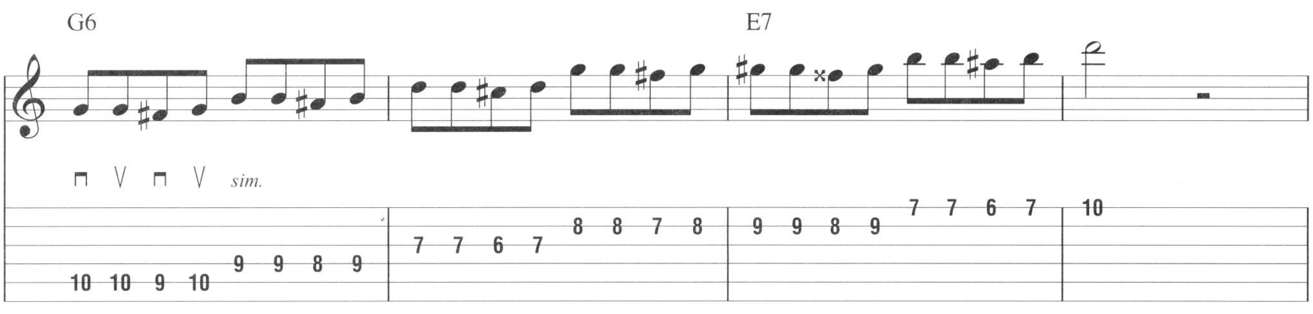

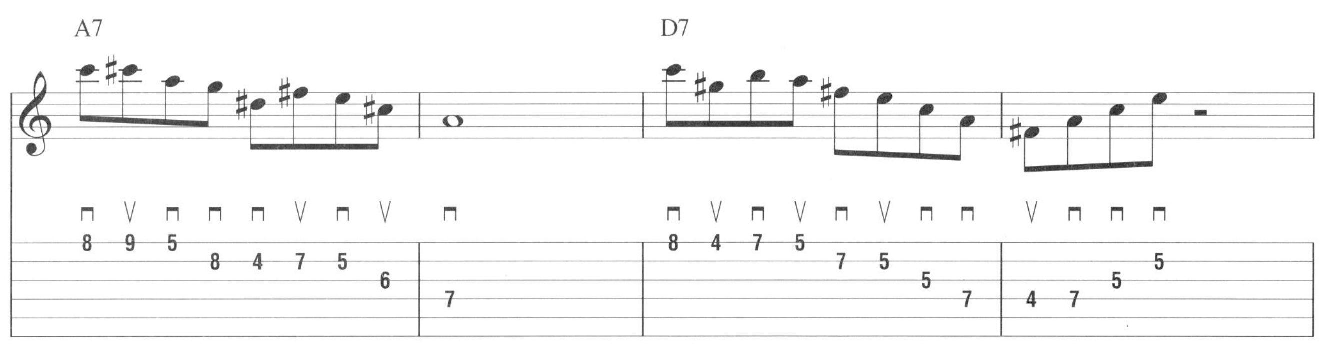

CHAPTER 6

SOLOING WITH CHROMATIC RUNS AND TRIPLETS

Chromatic Runs 

Being able to execute fast phrases is imperative in the Gypsy style, and using *chromatic runs* is a big part of getting that speed. Any two chord tones can be linked with a chromatic run, so this is where your knowledge of the arpeggios really pays off.

For these examples, we will again use our basic minor and major shapes for reference (tones from the shape that aren't used appear in white). By now, you should be familiar with the four different shapes, so I won't walk you through each chord. Be sure to take note of which tones are being linked in the chromatic runs. Our first example uses a chord progression similar to the A section of the tune "Swing Gitan."

FIG. 56

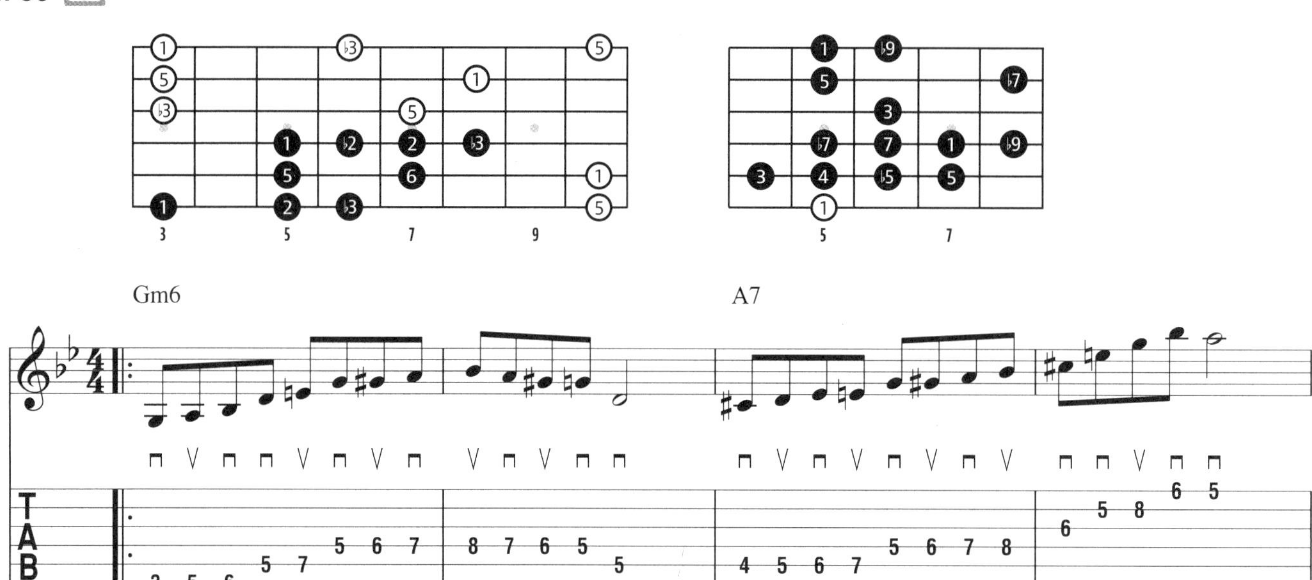

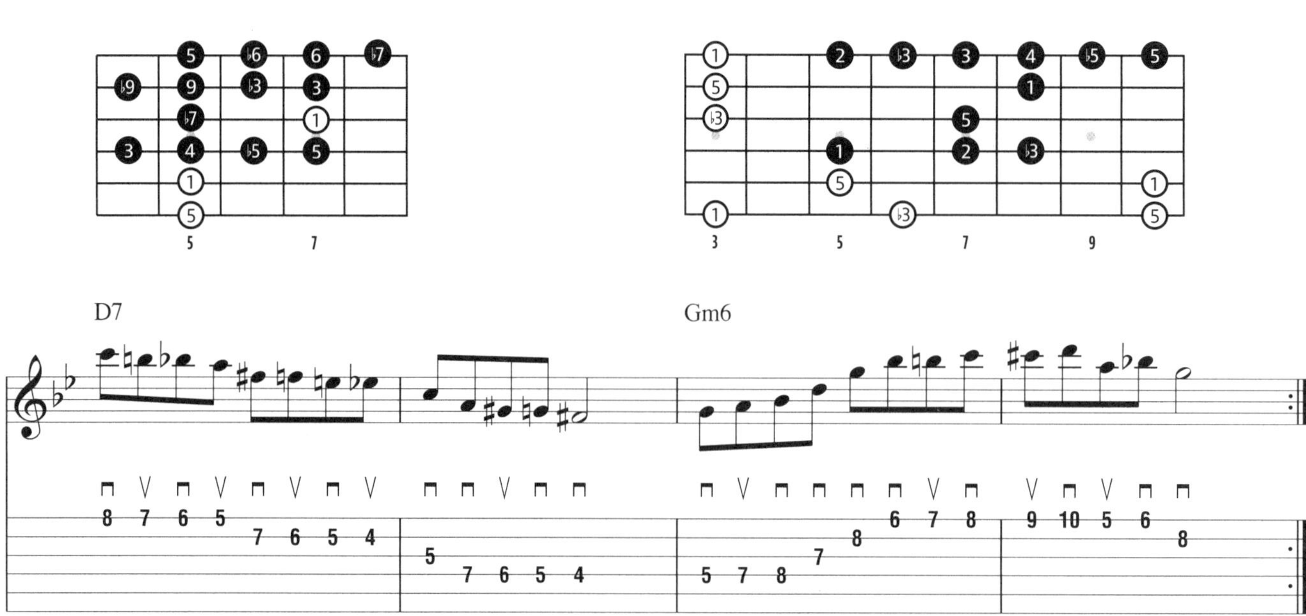

The second example uses a chord progression similar to the A section of the tune "Coquette."

FIG. 57

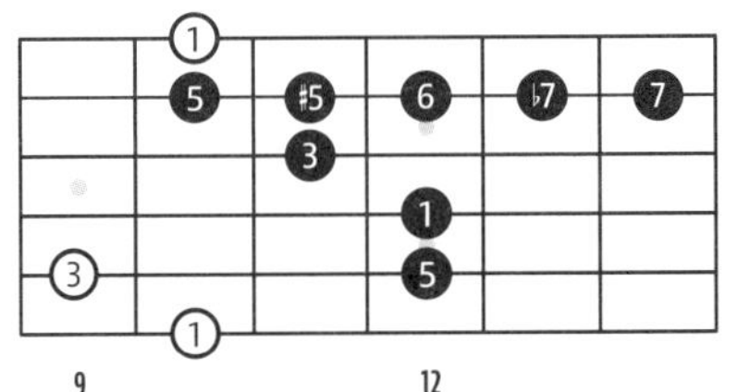
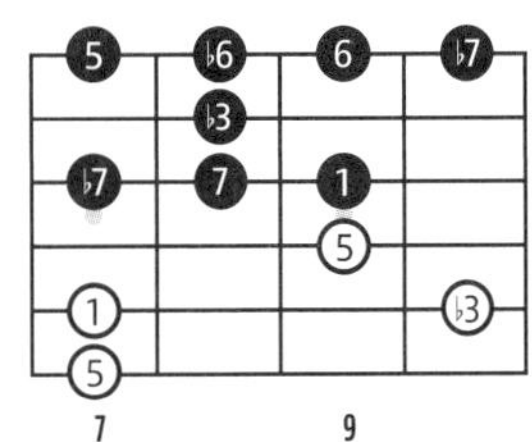
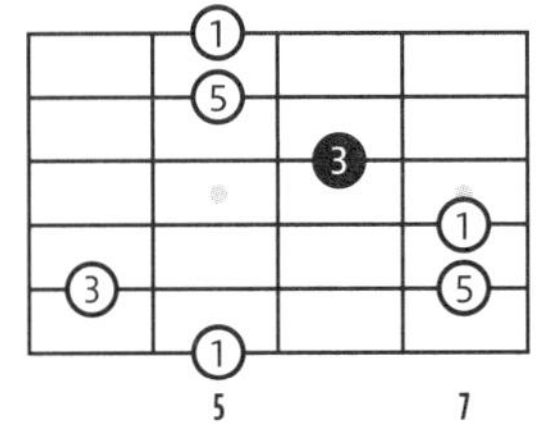
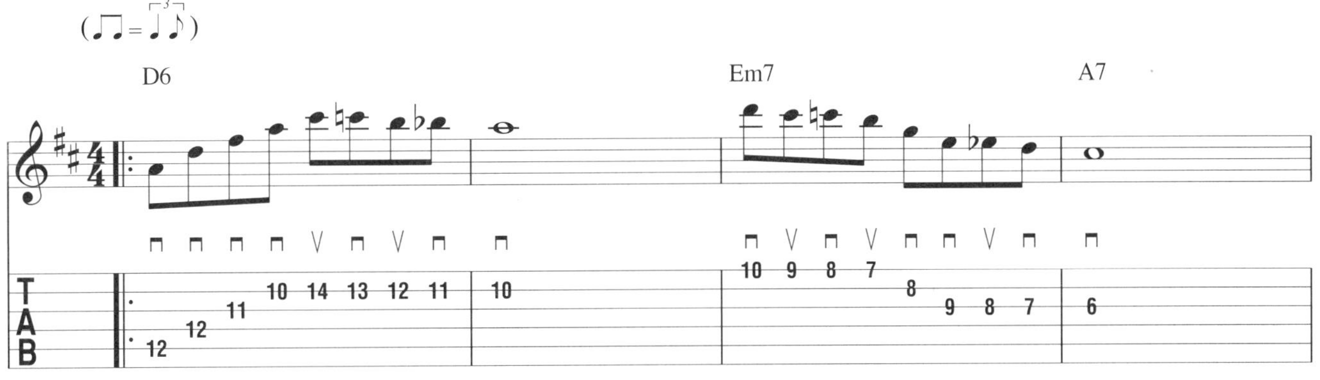

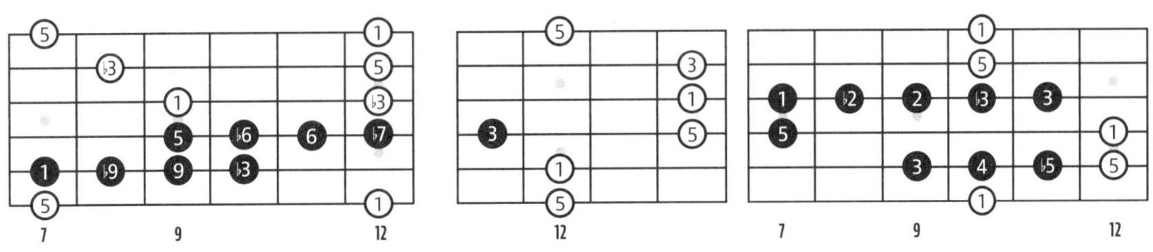
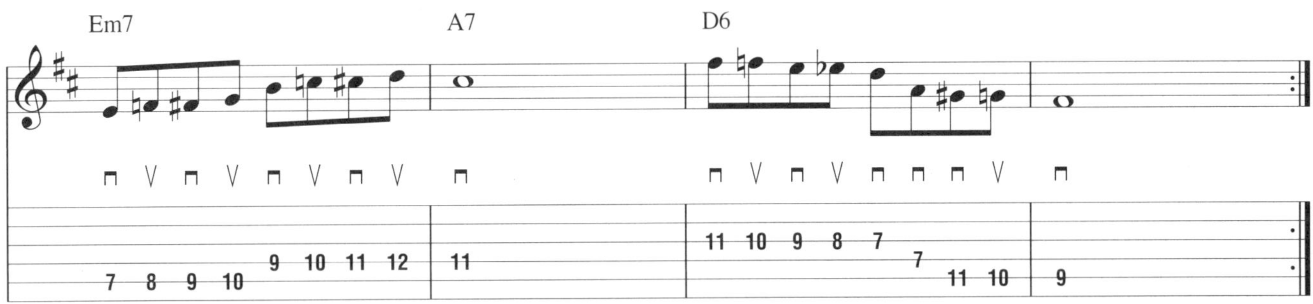

The third example uses a chord progression similar to the A section of the tune "Stompin' at Decca."

FIG. 58

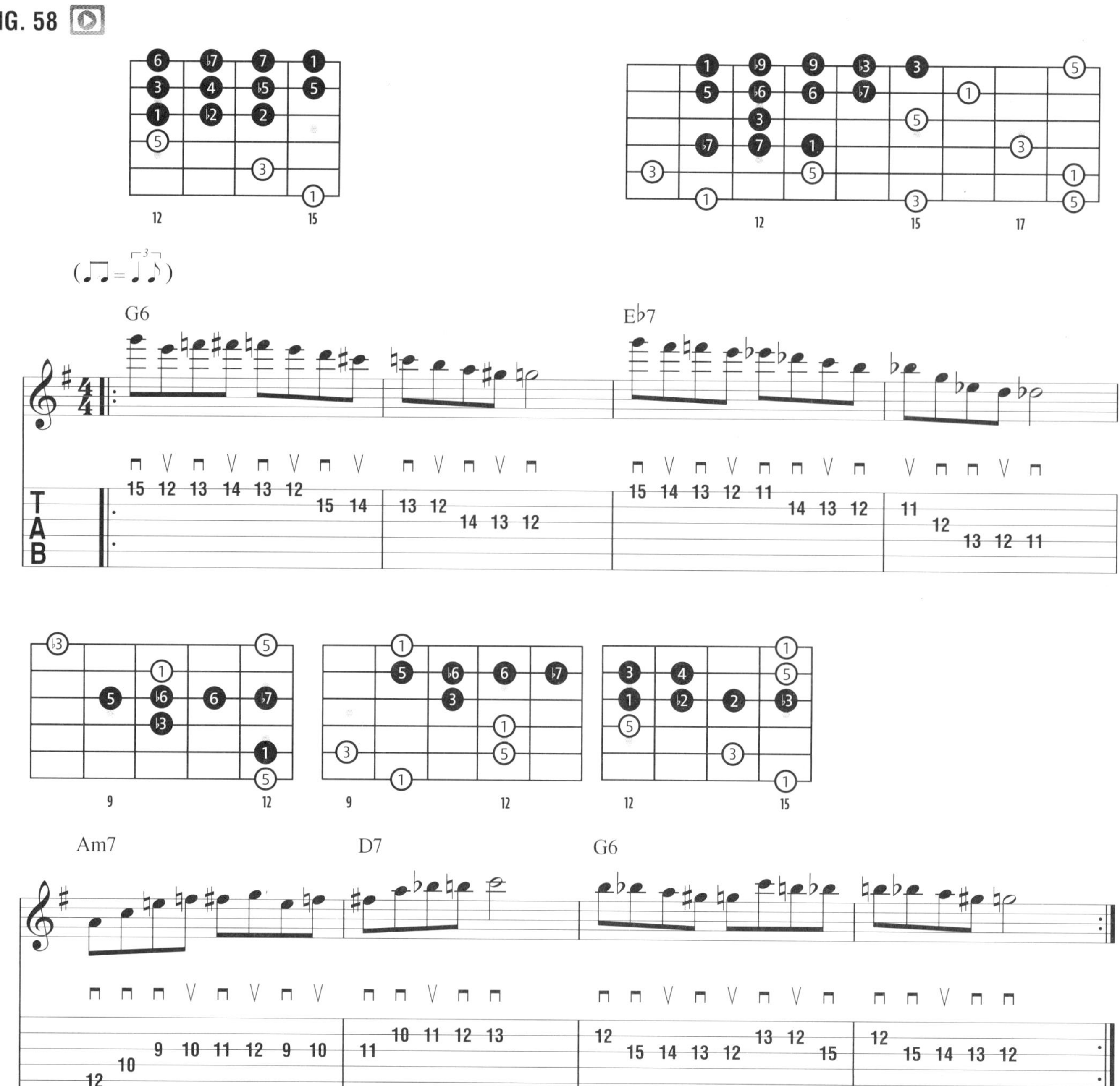

Long Chromatic Runs

So far, we have looked at short chromatic runs that span three or four frets, but it is also common to play much longer phrases, generally using open strings. These long chromatic runs are usually played as 16th or 32nd notes. In this first example, we'll play a chromatic run that spans four octaves starting on string 6 (E) and finishing on the E at fret 12, string 1. Though it might be counterintuitive for those of us that can make use of all four digits, playing this phrase with the two fingered approach à la Django is easier. The movement comes primarily from the forearm and not the fingers, which makes it easier to control, especially on string 1.

FIG. 59

Breaking It Down Slowly

It's best to take this one string at a time, counting in groups of five and four:

- String 6: 1–2–3–4–5
- String 5: 1–2–3–4–5
- String 4: 1–2–3–4–5
- String 3: 1–2–3–4
- String 2: 1–2–3–4–5
- String 1: 1–2–3–4–1–2–3–4–1–2–3–4–5

Gypsy players often use a variant on this chromatic run by just playing up to fret 3 on all strings. This one is a little easier to execute.

FIG. 60

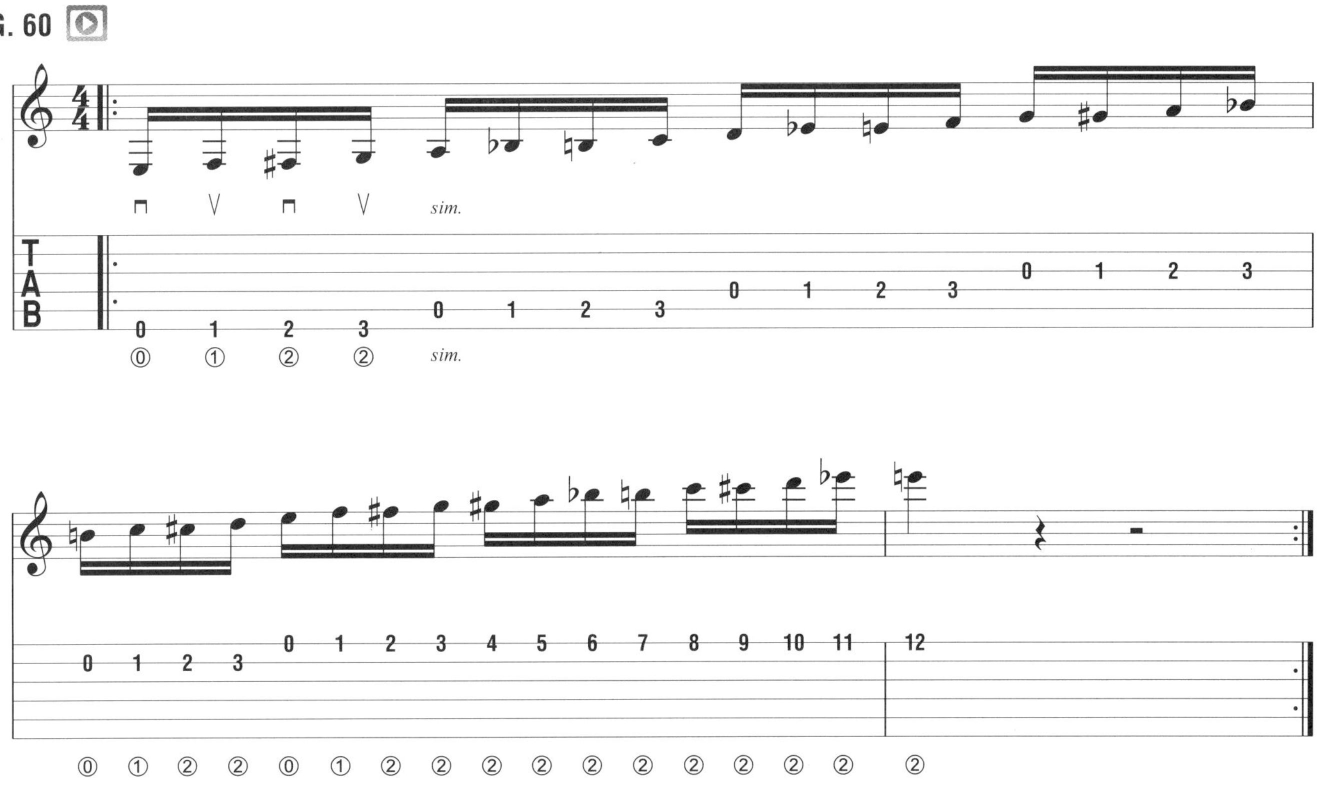

Our solo example will incorporate these chromatic runs along with neighboring tones and enclosures. We'll play over a chord progression similar to the tune "Dark Eyes." You'll remark that this solo starts with pick-ups, which means there are a few melody notes before the chords arrive on measure 1.

FIG. 61

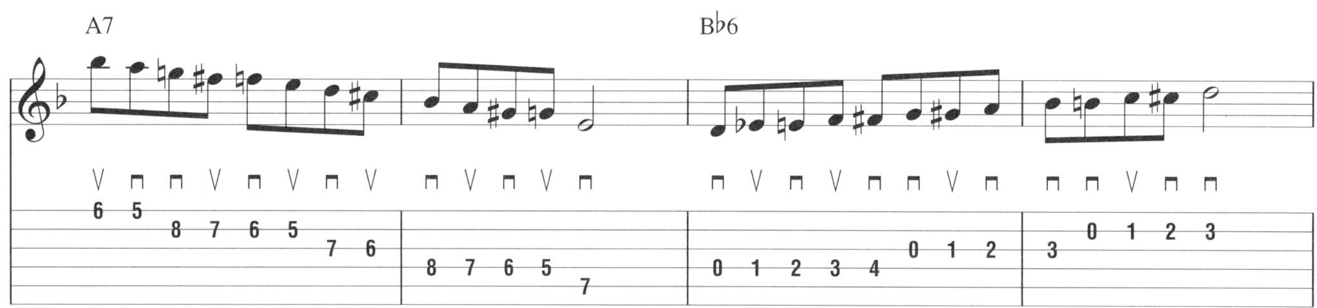

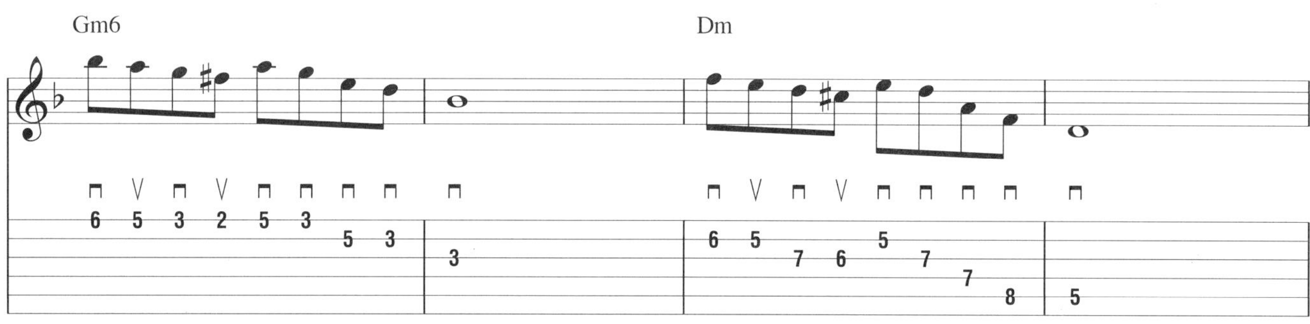

Triplets

Eighth-note triplets are a staple of Gypsy jazz soloing and one of the most important things to practice, as they often require double-down strokes.

This example uses a chord progression similar to the tune "Exactly Like You."

FIG. 62

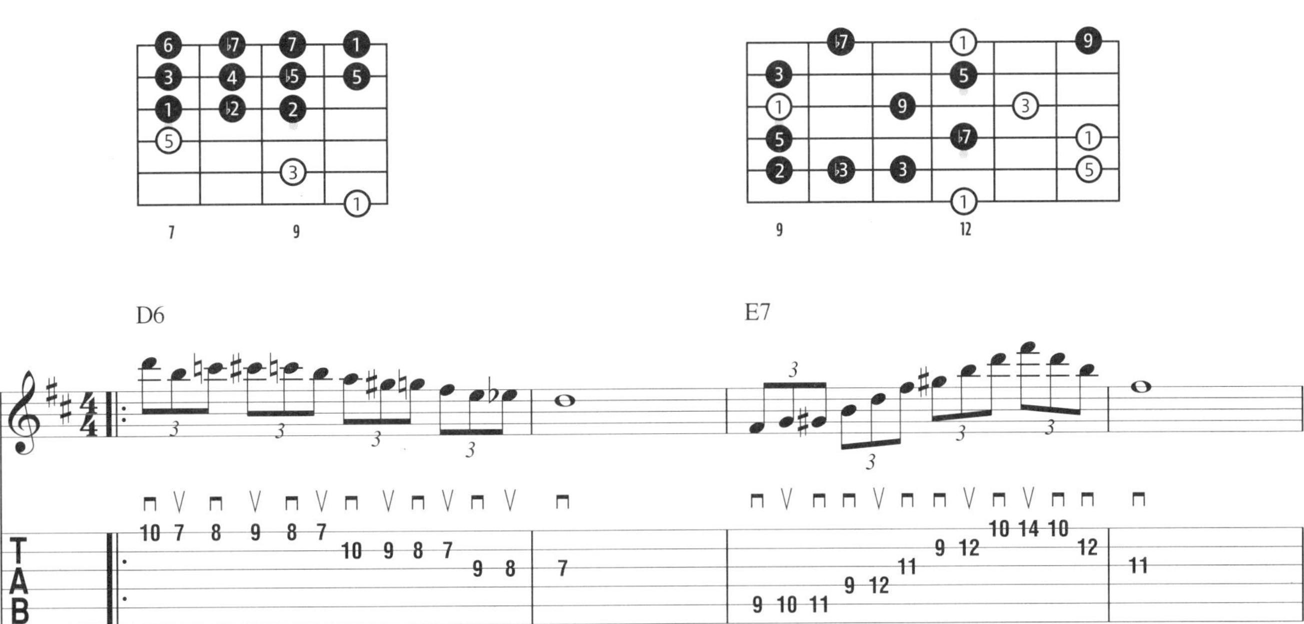

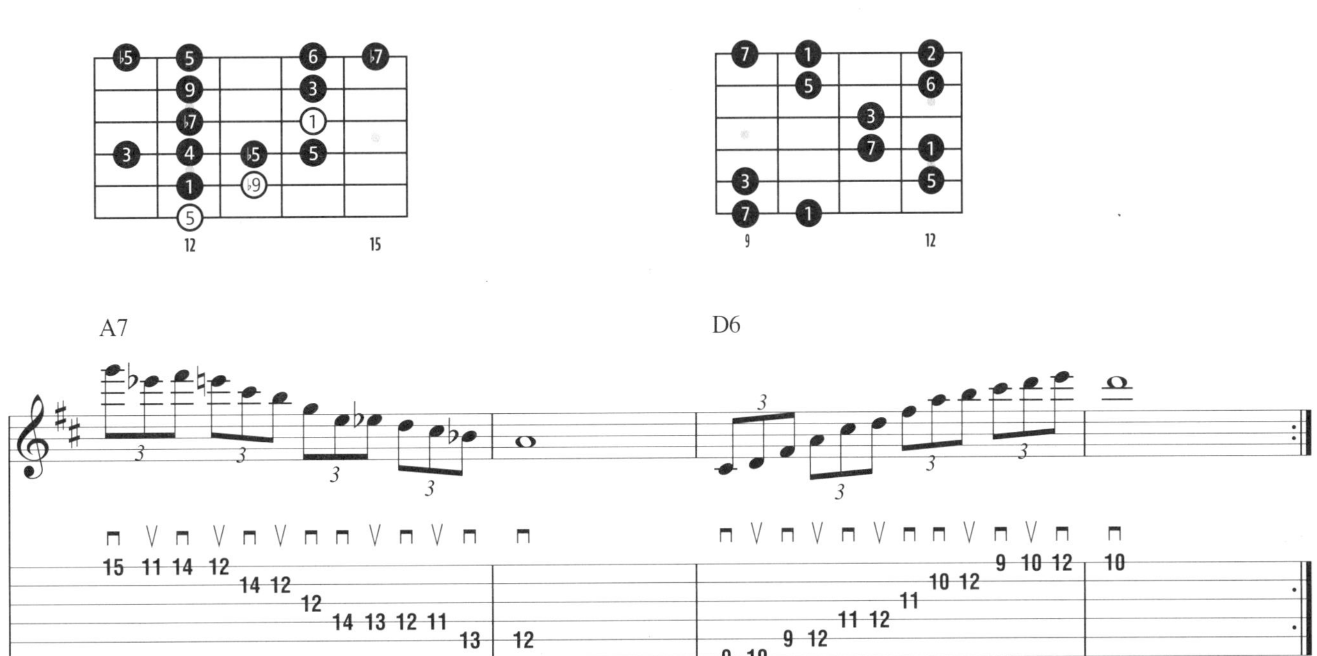

This example uses a progression similar to the A section from "Minor Swing."

FIG. 63

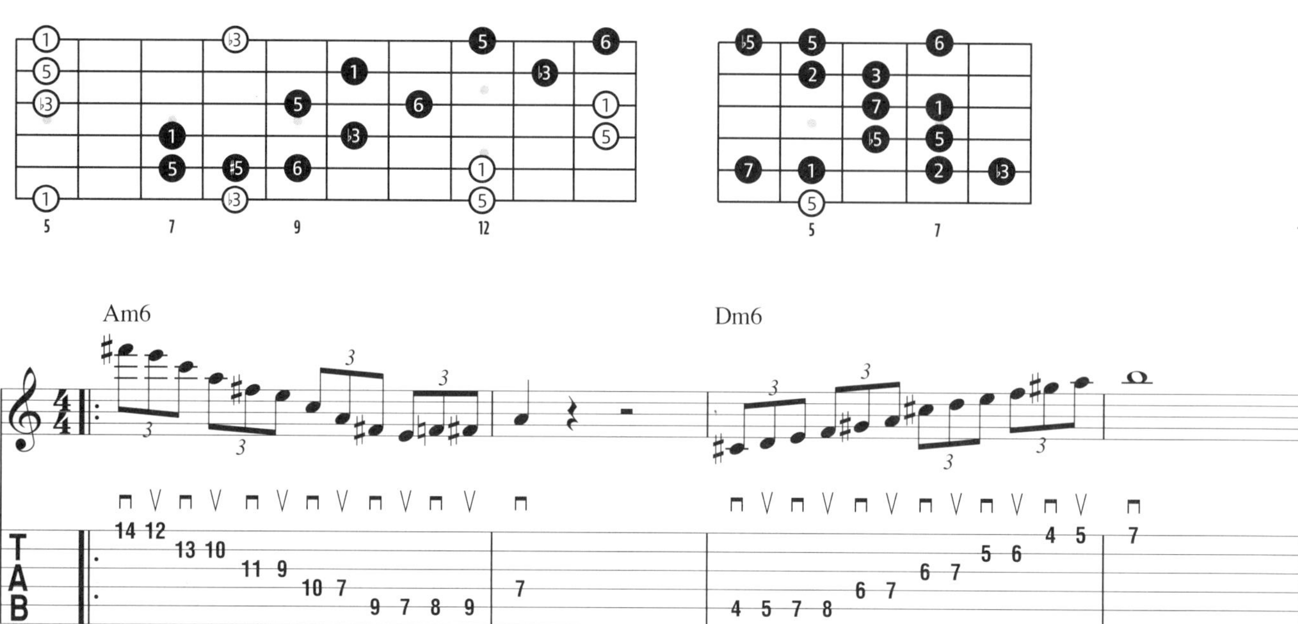

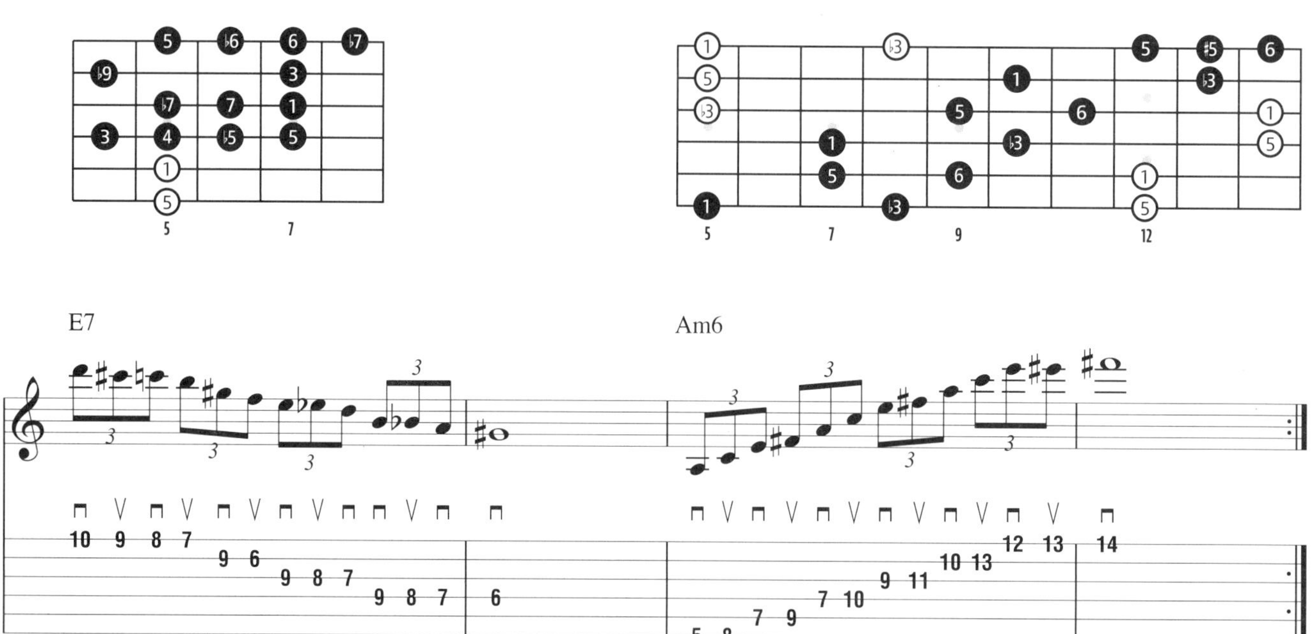

This example uses a progression similar to the A section of "Dinette."

FIG. 64

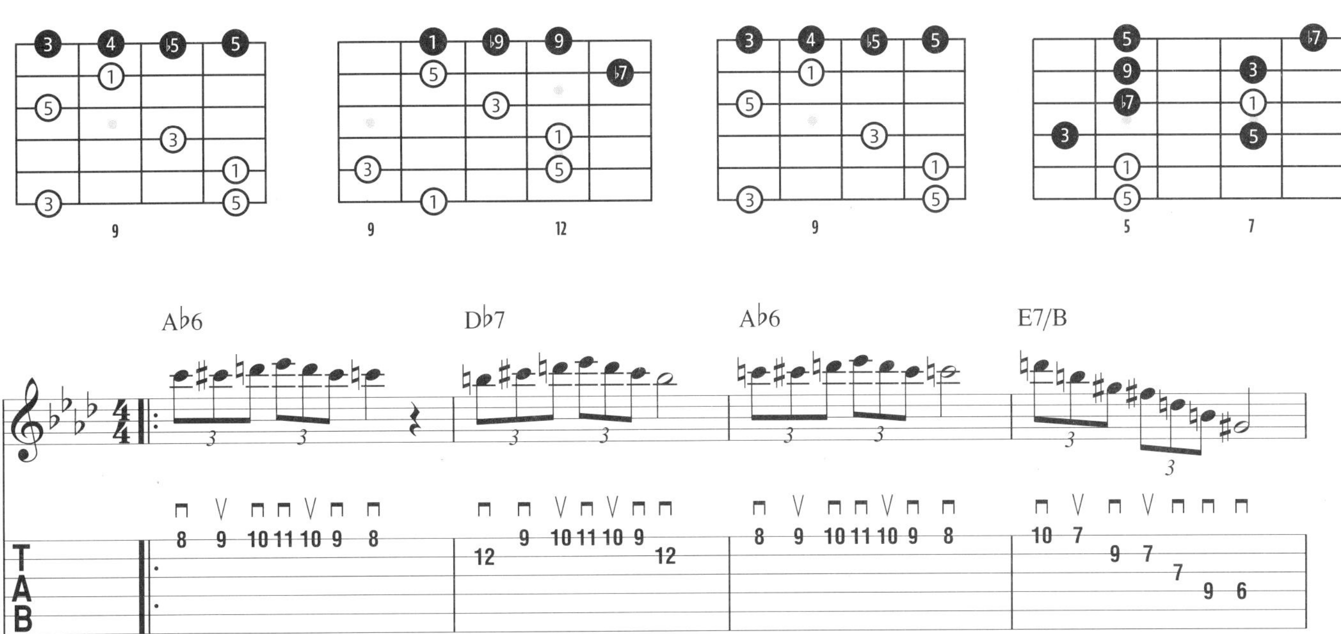

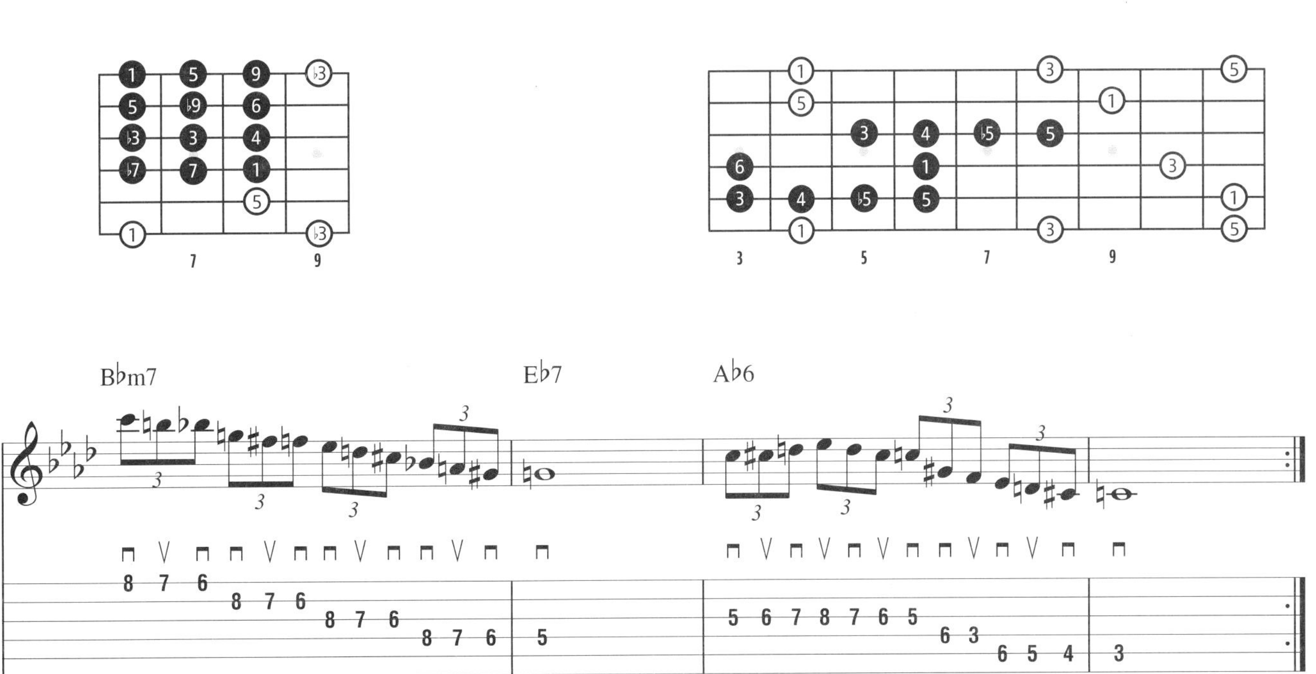

Our next solo example is played over chord changes similar to the tune "Bossa Dorado" and has a Gypsy bossa rhythm. We'll incorporate all thse techniques we've learned thus far. You'll see that there is a chord in this chart that we haven't yet encountered: the Em7♭5. This chord contains the same notes as a Gm6 chord, so we can treat it as such. (We'll discuss this chord in more detail later in the book.)

FIG. 65

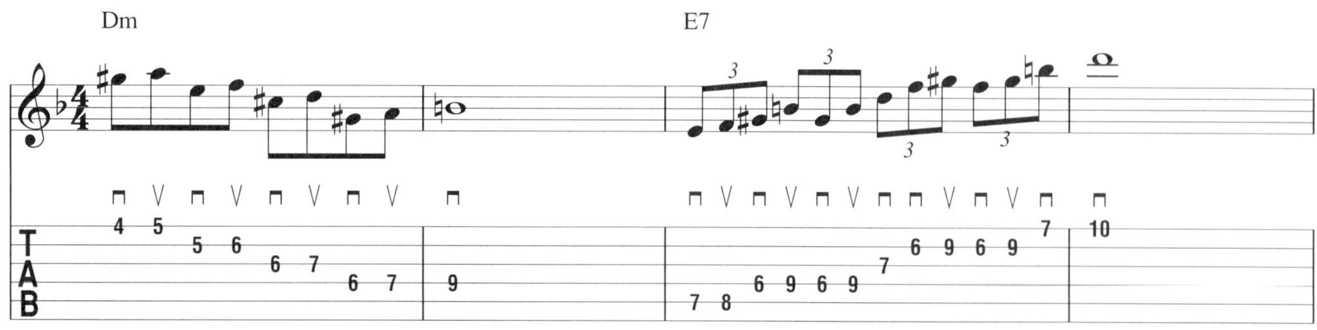

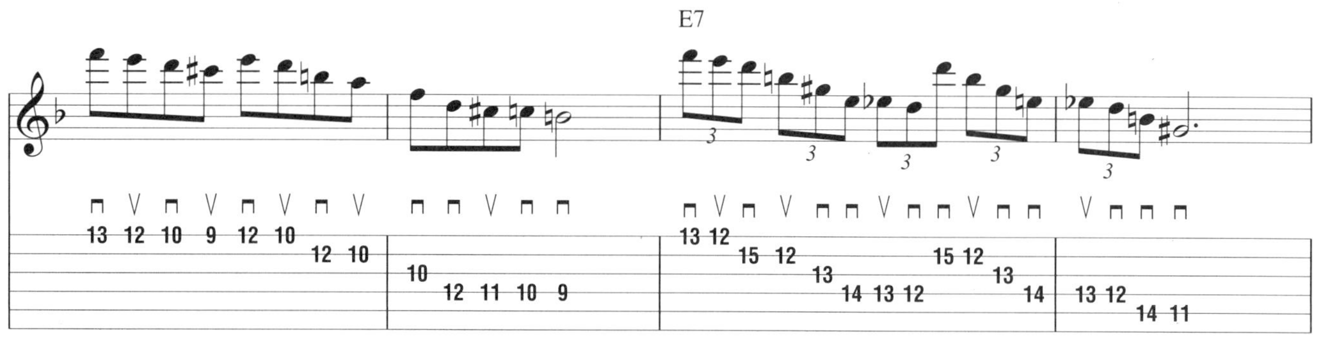

CHAPTER 7

ORNAMENTATION AND EMBELLISHMENTS

Anyone who's played blues or rock guitar will be familiar with the basic ornamentation of hammer-ons, pull-offs, slides, and string bends. These techniques are all used in Gypsy jazz but with a different approach that gives them a distinctive sound. All exercises are played with a swing feel.

Hammer-Ons and Pull-Offs

This first hammer-on/pull-off lick is fairly simple—basically an enclosure of the root (A). Pay close attention to the picking, though. In most styles, the note after the pull-off would be played by sliding into it. In Gypsy jazz, however, this note is generally picked with an up stroke. This lick is played over an Am chord.

FIG. 66

This is a great altered-chord lick that you hear a lot of modern players use. Here, it is played over an A7 chord.

FIG. 67

Here's one more hammer-on/pull-off lick, this time using enclosures over an A6 chord.

FIG. 68

String Bends

String bends are another technique that should be familiar to most guitarists. The majority of bends in Gypsy jazz are half steps, and the choice of notes is generally very different from what you'd hear in a blues or rock context.

In this lick over an A6 chord, we bend the ♭6th up to the 6th.

FIG. 69

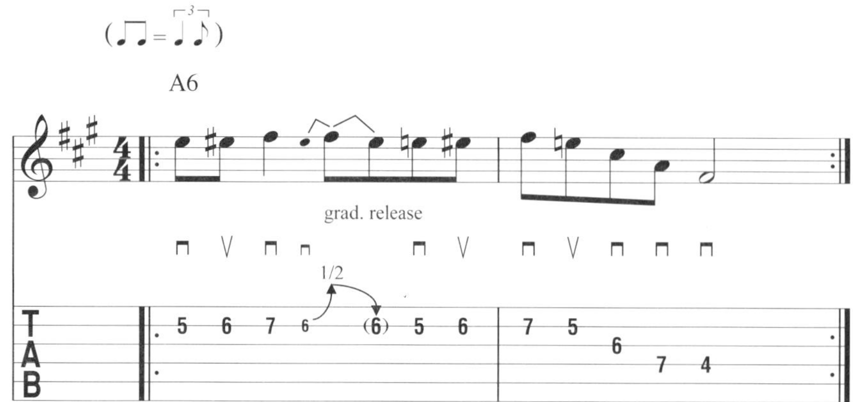

In this lick over a C6 chord, we bend the ♭5th up to the natural 5th.

FIG. 70

This lick over C7 combines both techniques. We start by bending the ♭9th up to the natural 9th and follow with a hammer-on and pull-off.

FIG. 71

Tremolo Picking

Tremolo picking is a technique used in many different styles and Django used this extensively, including sometimes on a single string…

FIG. 72

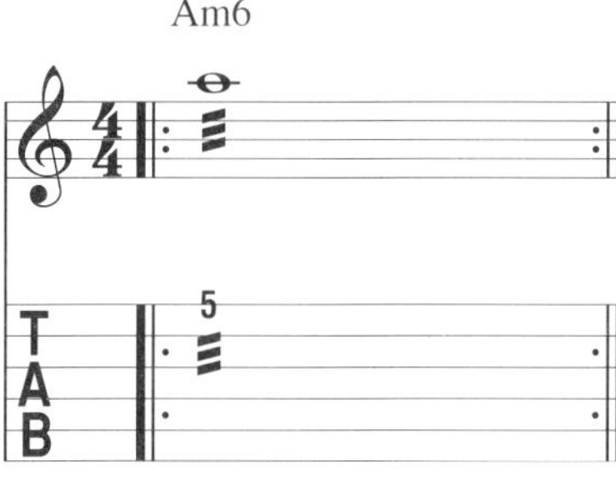

…and sometimes using a whole chord.

FIG. 73

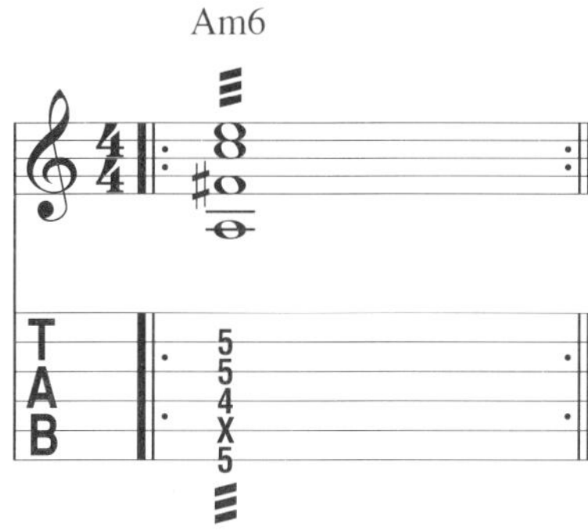

Slides

Some slides used in the Gypsy style are similar to what you might hear in a T-Bone Walker or Chuck Berry solo (playing one note on string 1 and then sliding into the same note on string 2, for example).

This example, played over an A6 chord, is inspired by a lick in the song "Django's Tiger." The target note is the second scale tone (B). It finishes with a bluesy hammer-on and pull-off.

FIG. 74

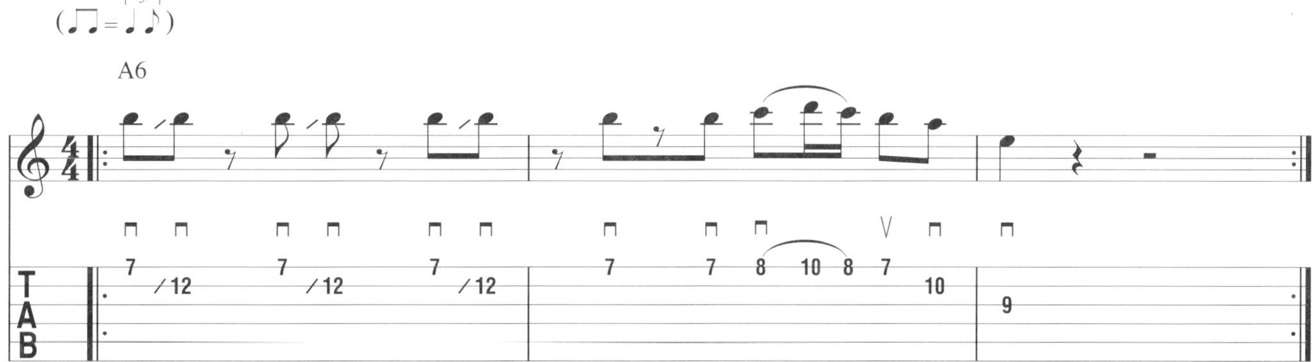

This example targets the root. The eighth notes are divided into groups of three, creating an interesting polyrhythmic effect.

FIG. 75

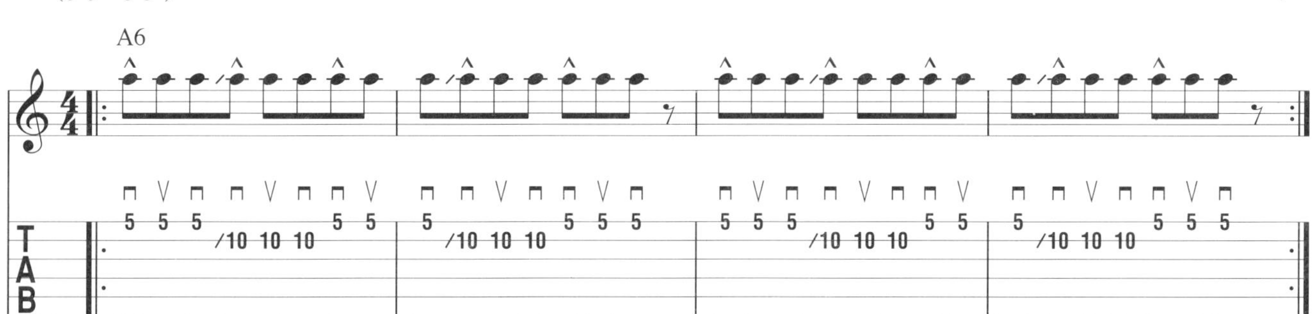

Django frequently played descending chromatic runs by sliding while playing 16th or 32nd notes. This example is over a Dm chord.

FIG. 76

This next example is over an A7 chord.

FIG. 77

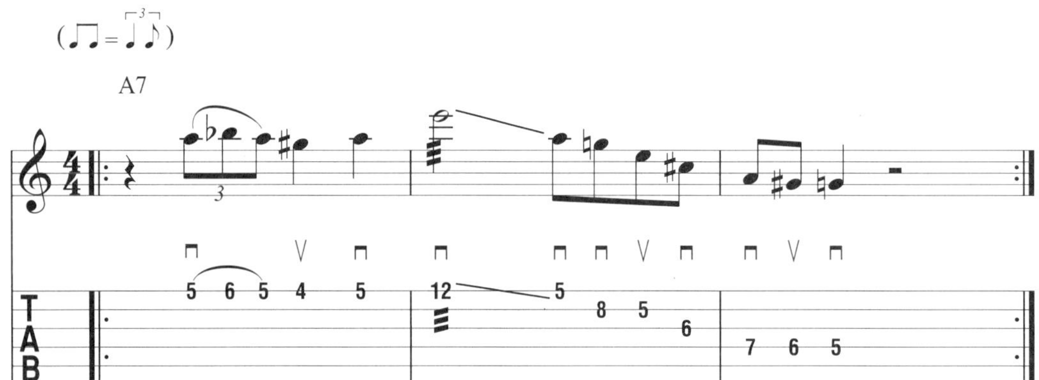

Chord Punctuation

Django would often "punctuate" a solo by playing a chord for one or two measures with a syncopated rhythm. Think of it as adding exclamation marks. Usually, the chord is approached from one or two frets below. In this example, we approach an A6/9 chord from two frets below with G6/9 and A♭6/9 chords.

FIG. 78

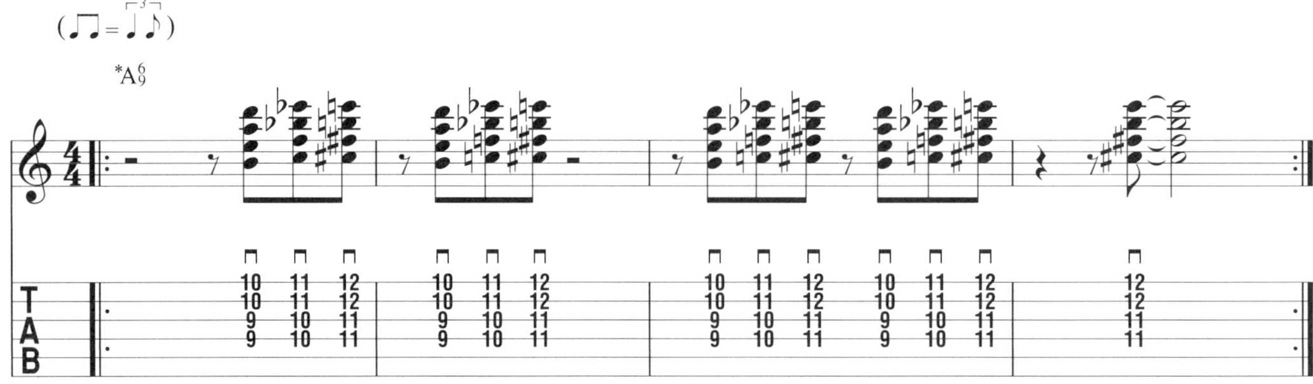

We'll now put these techniques into practice by playing a solo over chord changes similar to "Minor Swing."

FIG. 79

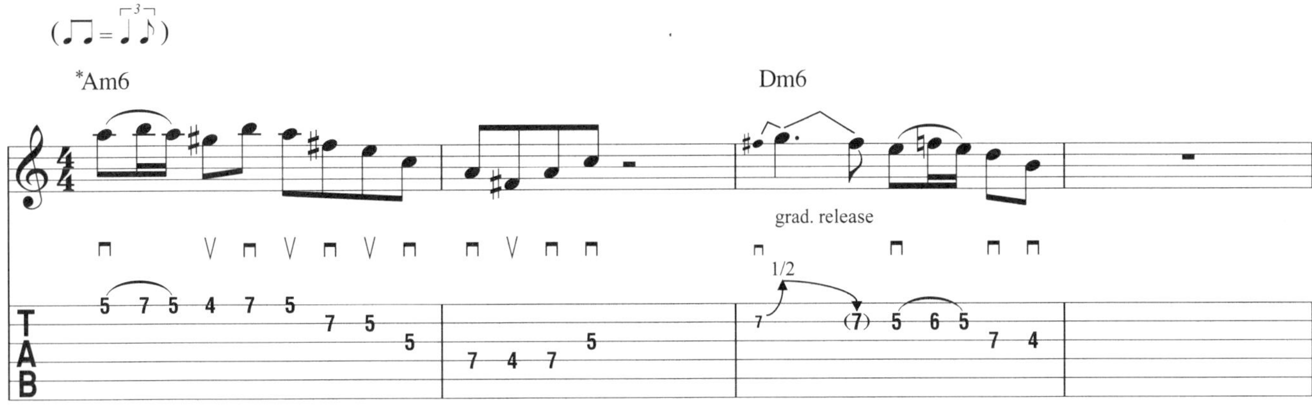

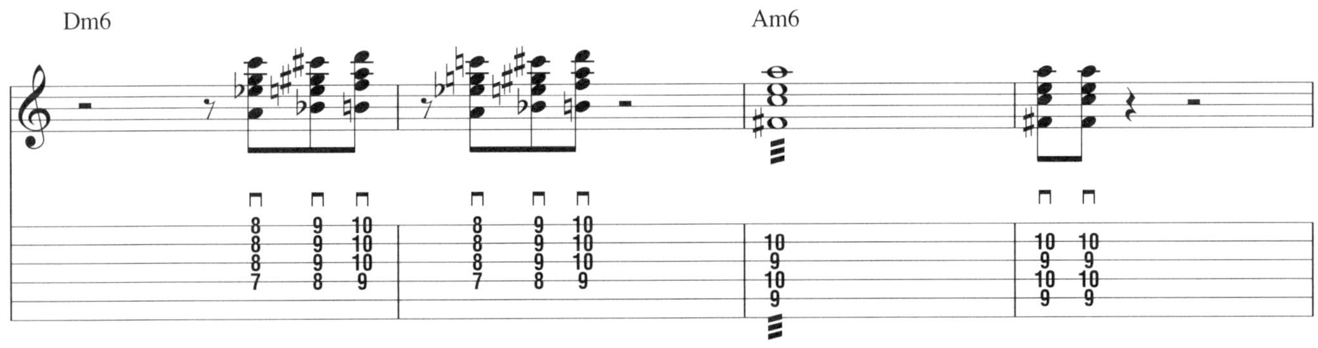

CHAPTER 8

SWEEP PICKING

Sweep picking (playing single notes on consecutive strings with a sweeping motion) is built into the Gypsy jazz style due to the frequent use of double-down strokes. These are generally short sweeps of two or three notes. Django did play longer sweeps occasionally, and today's players use the technique extensively.

We'll start with one of Django's iconic licks that you'll hear every player use. It's a series of diminished triads that function as dominant 7th voicings. Here, we are playing over an A7 chord. This is one of the few instances where we start a phrase with an up stroke.

FIG. 80

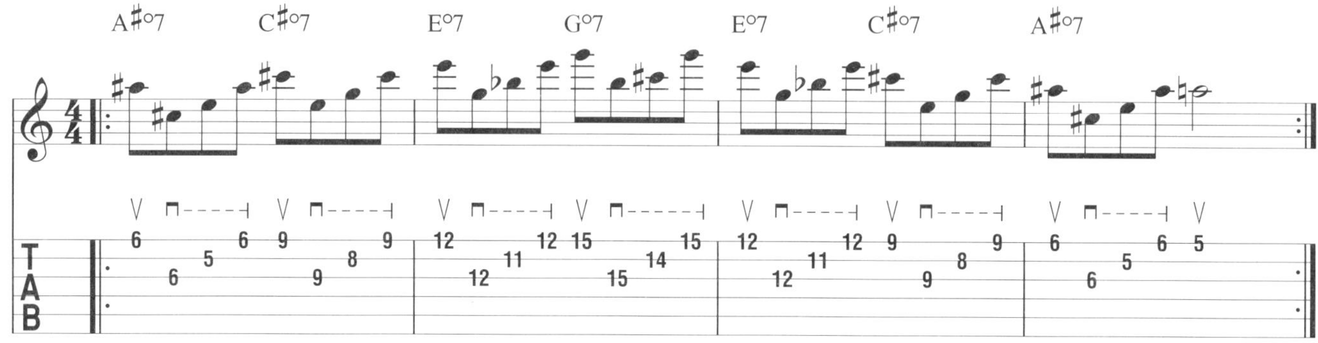

This example sweeps through a C6 arpeggio using major shape 4.

FIG. 81

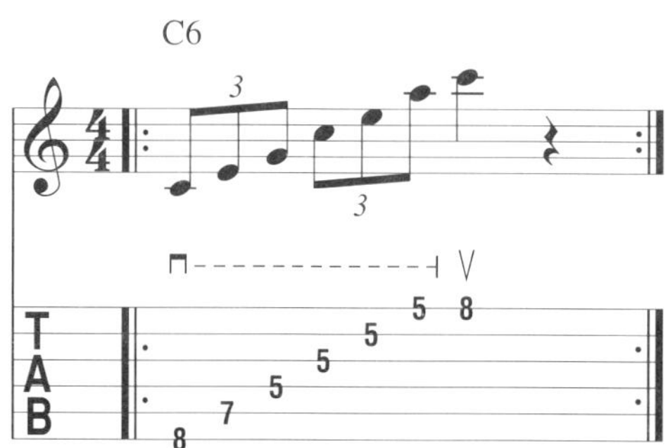

This next example sweeps through a Cm arpeggio using minor shape 4. This one is a little trickier, as there is an up stroke in the middle.

FIG. 82

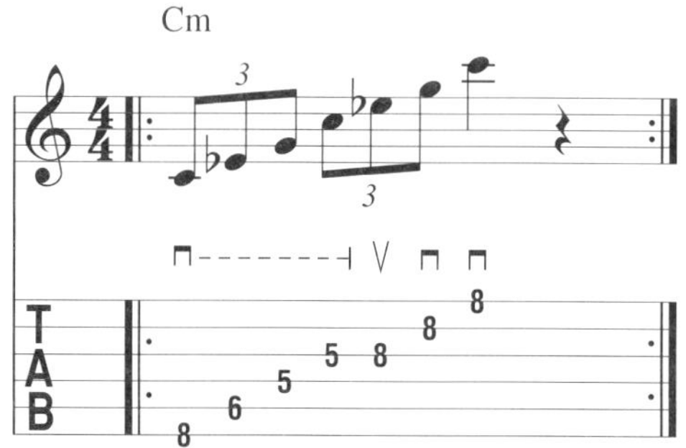

In this instance, we sweep through a G major arpeggio using major shape 2.

FIG. 83

This next part sweeps through a Gm arpeggio using minor shape 2.

FIG. 84

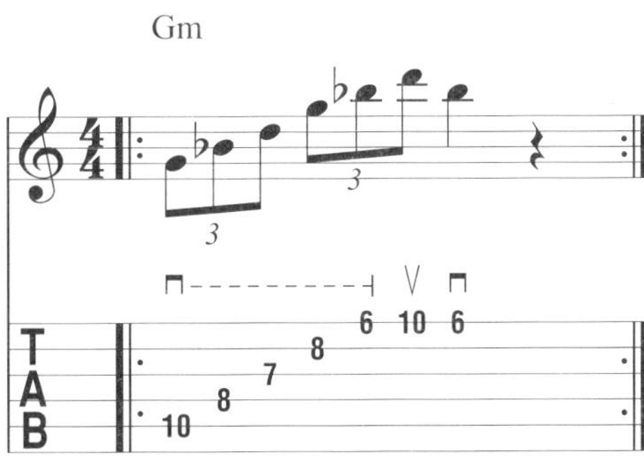

This figure is an alternative pattern for the same (Gm) arpeggio that allows you to finish in a higher register. I like to treat this as two separate, three-note sweeps. The alternative would be to use an up stroke on the note at fret 12 and sweep the next two notes.

FIG. 85

In the example on the next page, we sweep through a B♭6 arpeggio built around major shape 1. In the solo example, I use this same arpeggio to play over a Gm chord (the relative minor of B♭).

FIG. 86

Natural Sweep Picking

The following two examples are much shorter sweeps that occur naturally if you are following the picking rules. The first example is played over an A7 chord; the second one is played over an Am chord.

FIG. 87

FIG. 88

We'll now incorporate all these ideas into an example solo using a chord progression similar to the A section of "Swing Gitan," seen on the next page.

FIG. 89

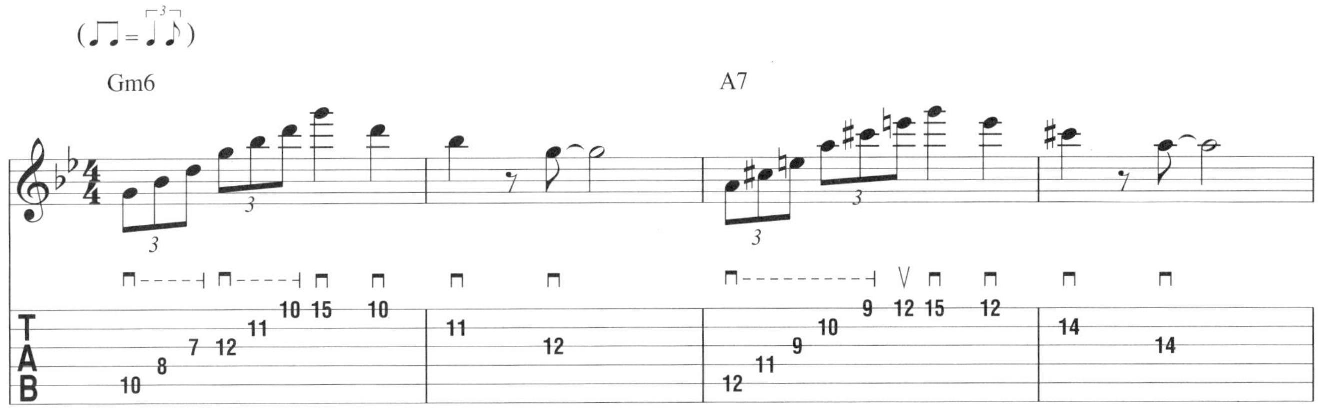

*Optional ending.

CHAPTER 9

MULTI-PURPOSE LICKS (PLURALITIES)

You may have noticed that we've used the same lick to play over different chord types in some of our exercises. We're now going to go deeper into the theory behind this in order to fully exploit it. We'll start by defining the term *plurality*. A plurality is a musical homonym: a group of notes that can function as multiple chords. A simple example of this would be the Am7 and C6 chords. They contain exactly the same notes, just in a different order.

- Am7 = A–C–E–G
- C6 = C–E–G–A

This means any C6 voicing can function as an Am7 chord and vice-versa, assuming the bass player plays the appropriate root. And, since the voicings are interchangeable, so are their arpeggios. Understanding this concept can make it simpler to play over complex chords. Take the Em7♭5 chord, for example. That might seem a little daunting to solo over until you realize that it contains the same four notes as a Gm6 chord.

- Em7♭5 = E–G–B♭–D
- Gm6 = G–B♭–D–E

There are two more common pluralities for a minor 6 voicing: the dominant 9th chord and the dominant 7th (♯5♭9). The root is absent from these voicings. It is likely being played by the bassist, but even if that's not the case, the ear recognizes them from the context of the chord progression. In the following examples, we'll use an arpeggio built around this chord form as a multi-purpose lick.

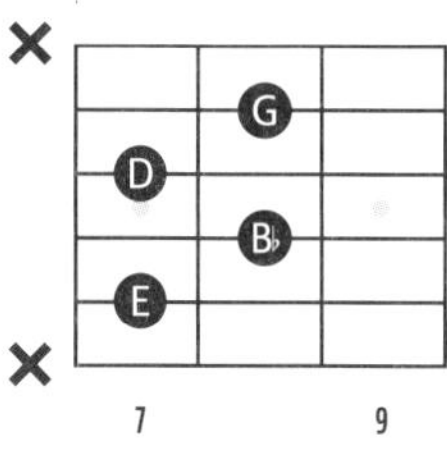

Pay close attention to the shifting identities of the tones as we change chord types. In this first example, we use the arpeggio over a Gm6 chord resolving to a Cm chord. Notes belonging to the chord form are circled.

FIG. 90

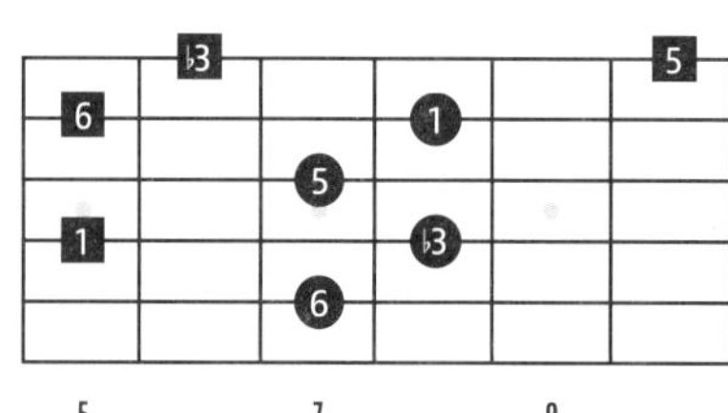

Now, we'll use the same arpeggio as a C9 resolving to an Fmaj7 chord.

FIG. 91

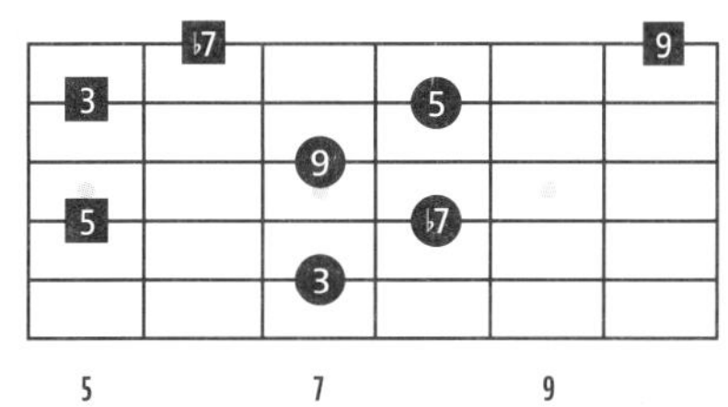

Here, we'll use the arpeggio over Em7♭5 moving to an A7 chord.

FIG. 92

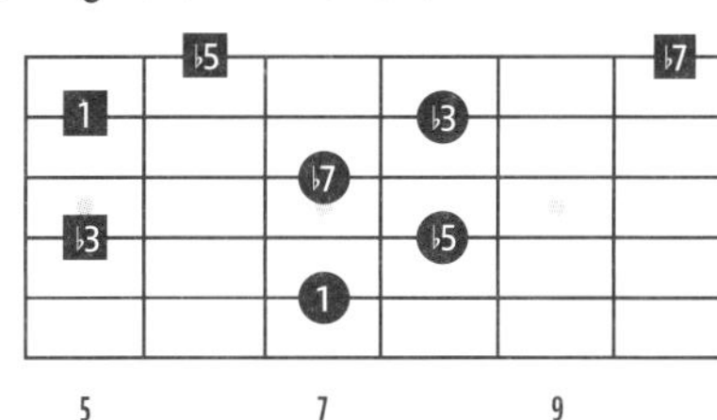

Exploring Further

For the final incarnation of this arpeggio, we'll use it as an F♯7♯5♭9 lick resolving to a Bm chord.

FIG. 93

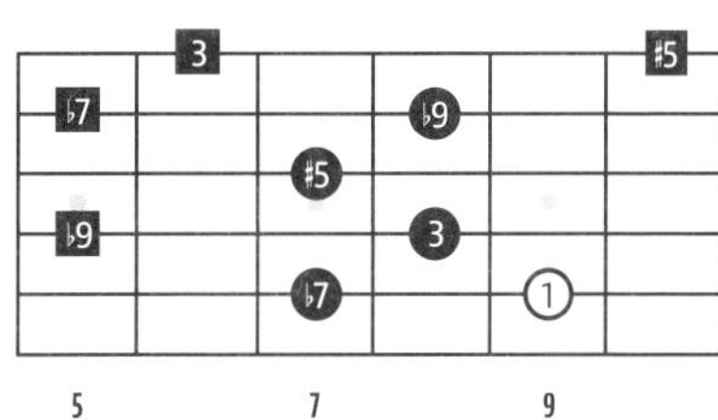

In these examples, we'll follow the same procedure, but use a different chord form.

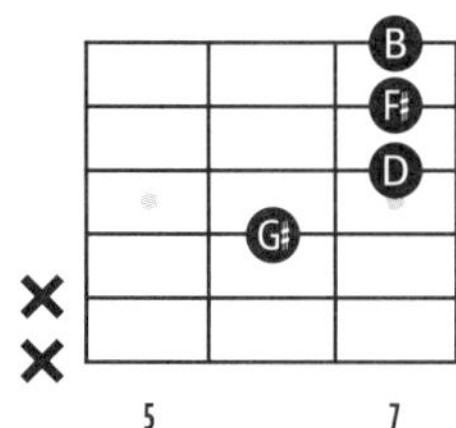

The first example is a Bm6 arpeggio resolving to an Em chord.

FIG. 94

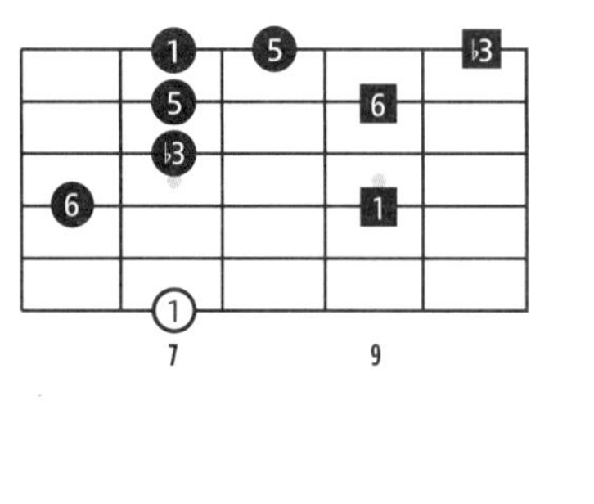

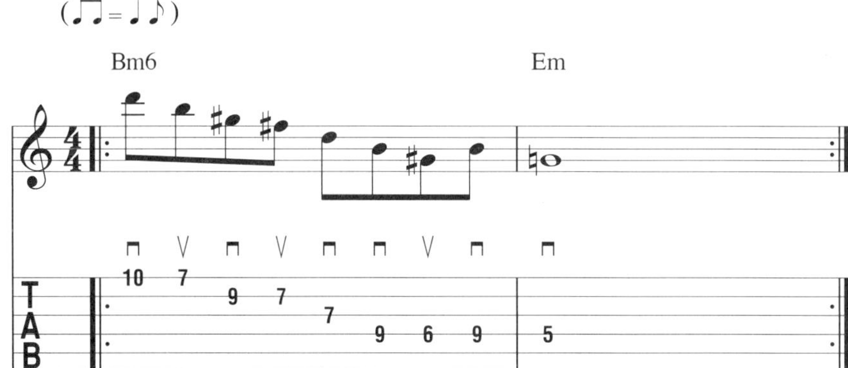

Now, we'll use the arpeggio over E9 resolving to an A6 chord.

FIG. 95

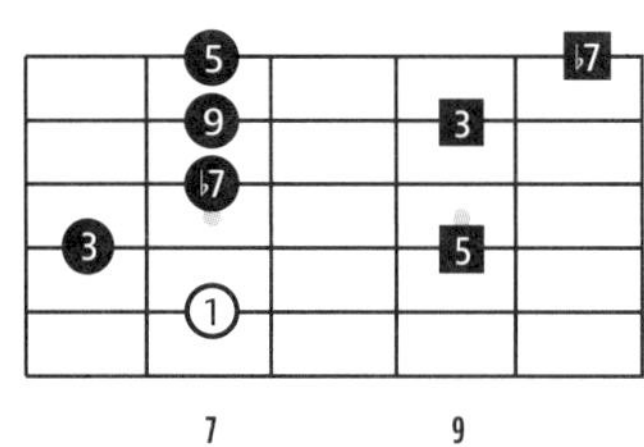

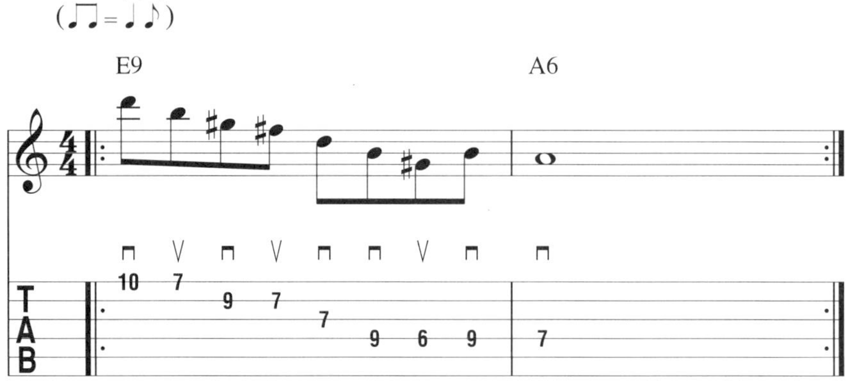

Here, we'll use the arpeggio over G♯m7♭5 moving to a C♯7 chord.

FIG. 96

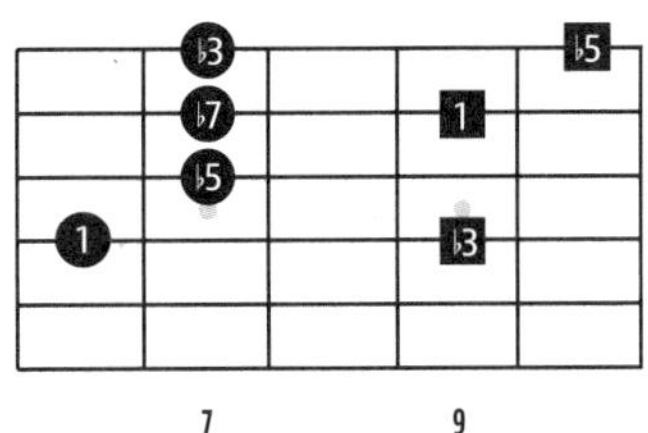

In this last example, the arpeggio functions as a B♭7 altered lick resolving to E♭maj7.

FIG. 97

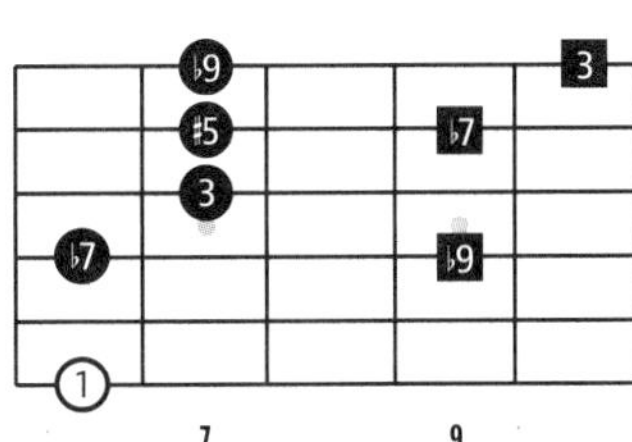

We'll now use these multi-purpose licks in the context of a solo.

FIG. 98

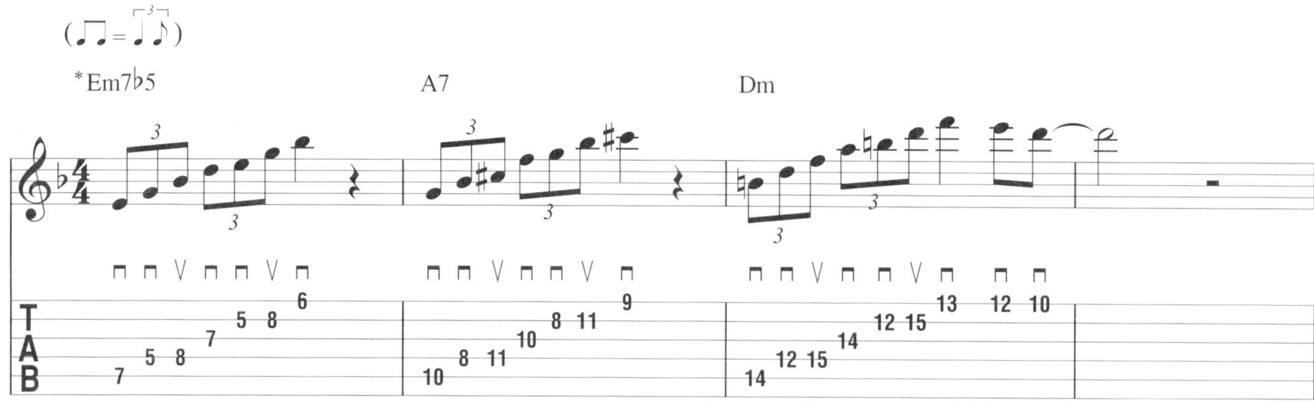

*Chord symbols reflect overall harmony.

CHAPTER 10

INTROS AND OUTROS

Now that you've learned the basic rhythm and lead techniques, we need to cover one last subject: how to start and finish a song. Some songs have specific intros and outros, but in many cases, players use a simple cadence or phrase that can be applied to any number of pieces. We'll examine some of the most common intros and outros in this section.

The introduction establishes the tempo and feel of a song. Most are four or eight measures long and use a simple cadence that navigates from the I chord to the V chord. The following examples could be used as intros for a song in C major. Make sure you can transpose them to any key.

Major Key Intros

FIG. 99

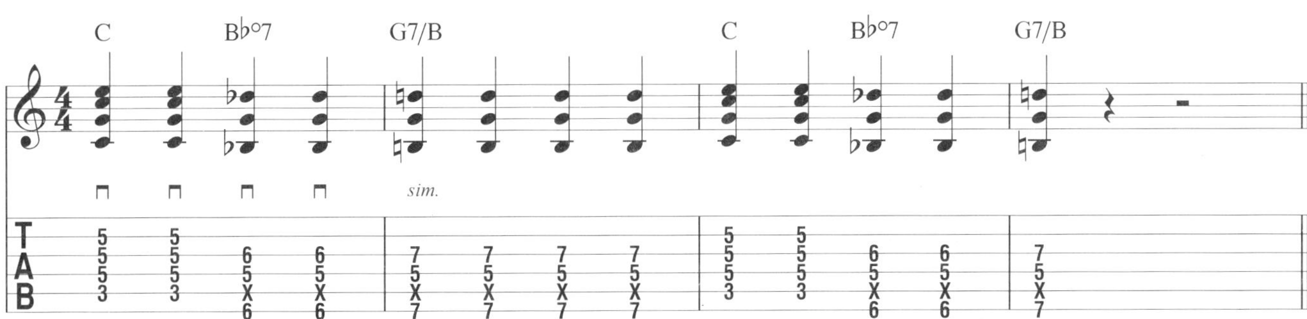

FIG. 100

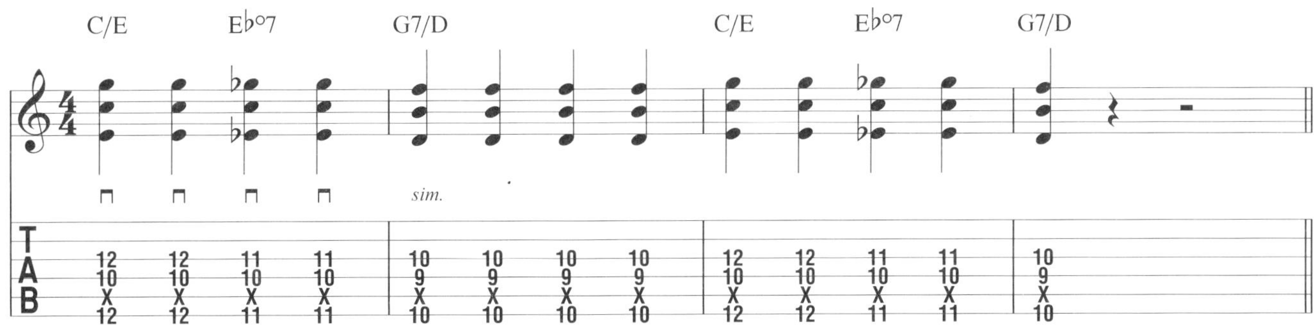

FIG. 101

Minor Key Intros

Intros for songs in a minor key follow the same principle (a cadence that moves from I to V), but here, obviously, the I chord is minor. The following examples could be used for a song in G minor.

FIG. 102

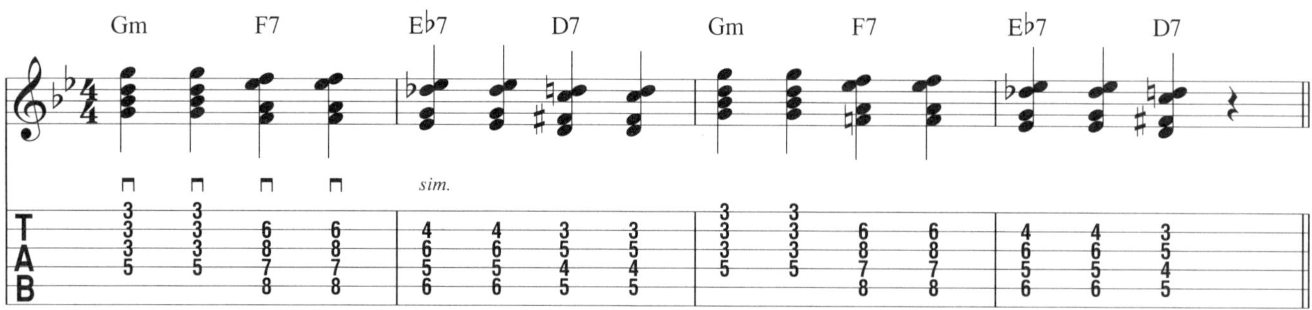

FIG. 103

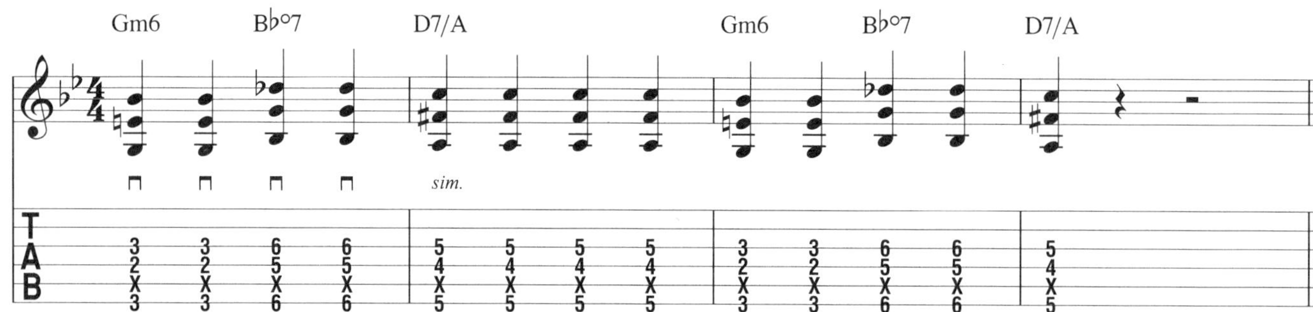

FIG. 104

Major Key Outros

Outros tend to be shorter (usually just two measures) and a little more flexible than intros. The Hot Club of France used the same ending for many tunes whether they were in a major or minor key. The following examples could be used for a song in D major beginning with the next figure.

FIG. 105

This chromatic run can also be played with full chords.

FIG. 106

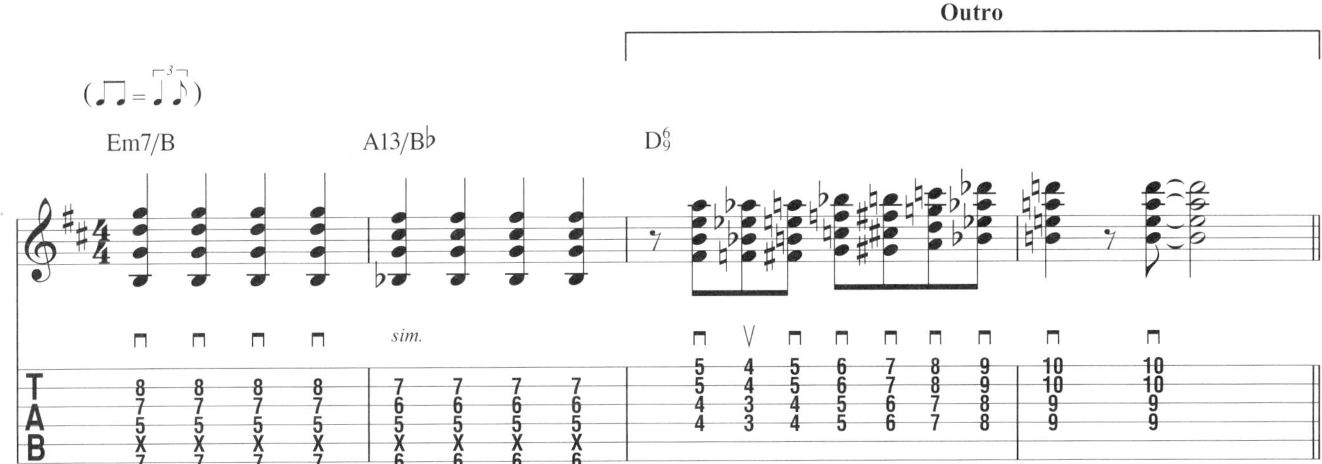

Another popular outro in a major key is to descend the major scale with a chromatic variation at the end.

FIG. 107

Minor Key Outros

Now, we'll look at some outros typically used in minor keys. In our first example, we use the same chromatic outro from before but played in octaves.

FIG. 108

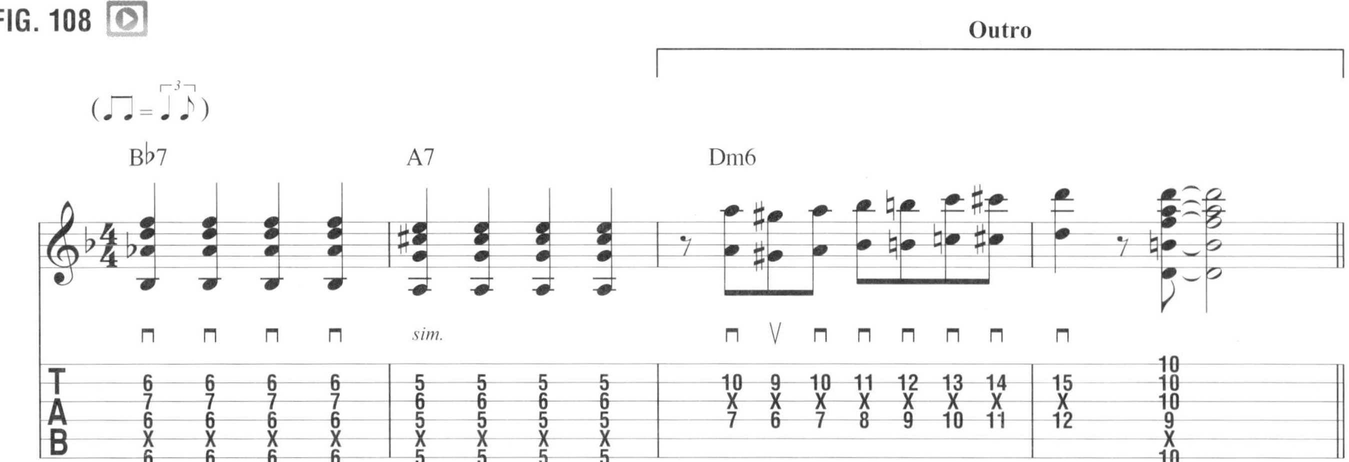

Another common ending is to play an arpeggio of the I chord followed by a diminished arpeggio starting one half step below that resolves back to I. There are lots of possible variations. Here are two:

FIG. 109

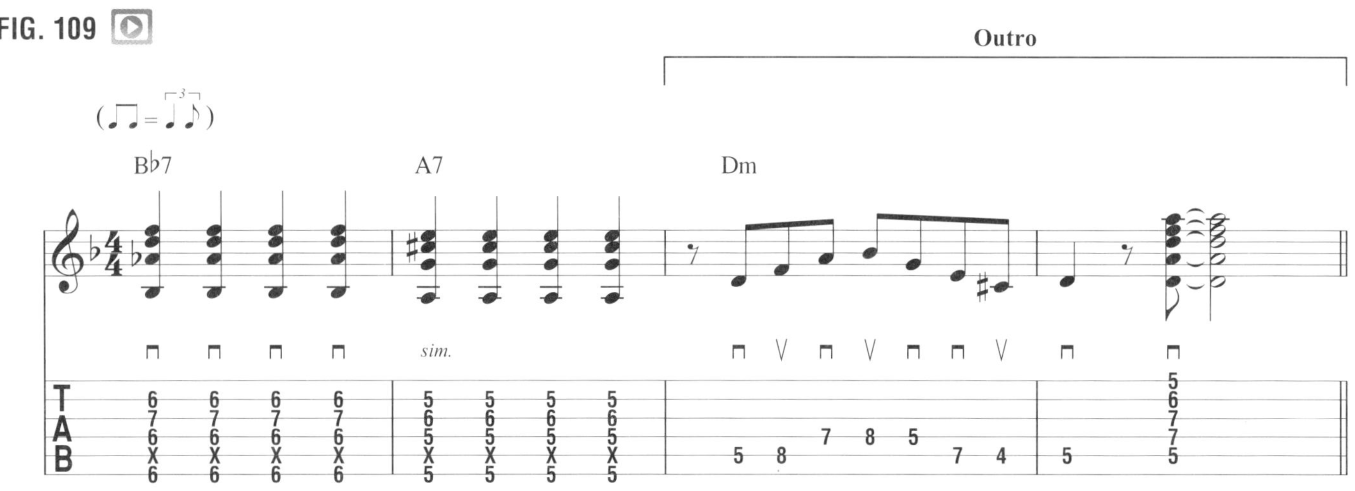

FIG. 110

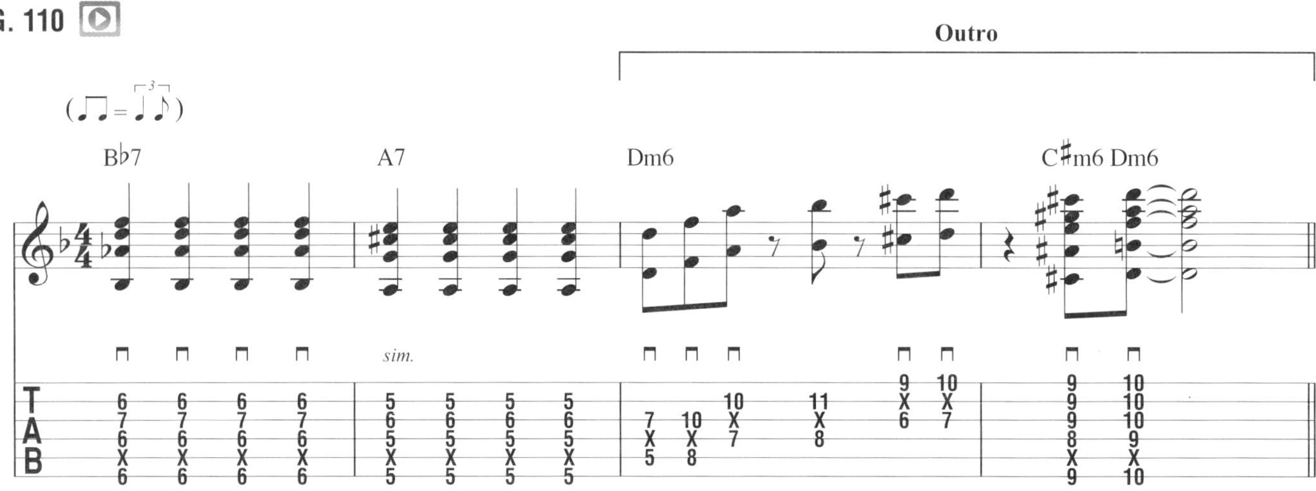

Once you've understood the concept behind these intros and outros, it's fairly easy to come up with new ones yourself. Like everything else in this book, I've tried to demonstrate the basic principles and guidelines. The real work and fun is to make them your own.

CHAPTER 11

SOLO EXAMPLES

In this section, you'll learn ten short solos that incorporate all of the concepts we've studied. The chord progressions are all based on popular tunes from the repertoire. You should also use these tracks to practice your rhythm playing. I've used some common chord substitutions and alternate voicings that you should incorporate into your vocabulary.

Solo 1

Solo 1, seen on the following page, is based on the chord changes to "Minor Swing."

Chords Used

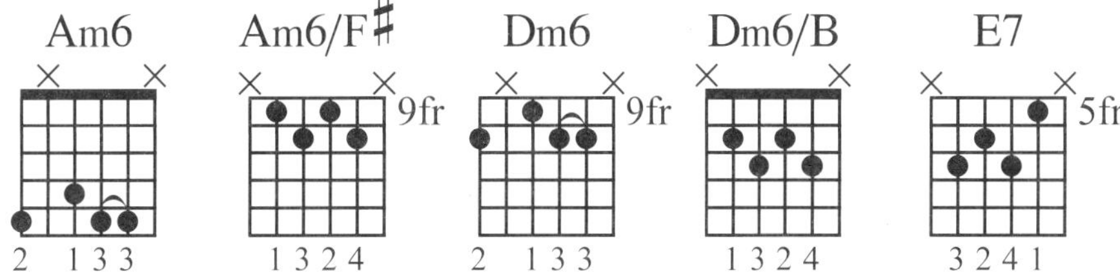

Rhythm

Note the alternate minor 6 chord voicing used in measures 3 and 4 (Dm6/B), and measures 11 and 12 (Am6/F♯). You should recognize this chord from the pluralities chapter.

Solo Breakdown

- Measures 1 and 2: The ubiquitous Django enclosure lick.
- Measures 3 and 4: A half-step bend from the 3rd to the 4th followed by a hammer-on and pull-off lick.
- Measures 5 and 6: I outline an E7♭9 chord.
- Measures 7 and 8: A simple enclosure idea over which I superimpose an A7♭9 lick over the Am chord. Notice that the A7♭9 lick doesn't start until the second half of measure 8. It's anticipating the arrival of the Dm chord. If it was started too early, it would clash.
- Measures 9 and 10: A Dm6 arpeggio using some chromatic passing tones.
- Measures 11 and 12: A hammer-on/pull-off enclosure lick followed by a typical Django bend—the ♭9 to 9.
- Measures 13 and 14: A long E7♭9 arpeggio linked with chromatic tones.
- Measures 15 and 16: A standard ending from the intros and outros section.

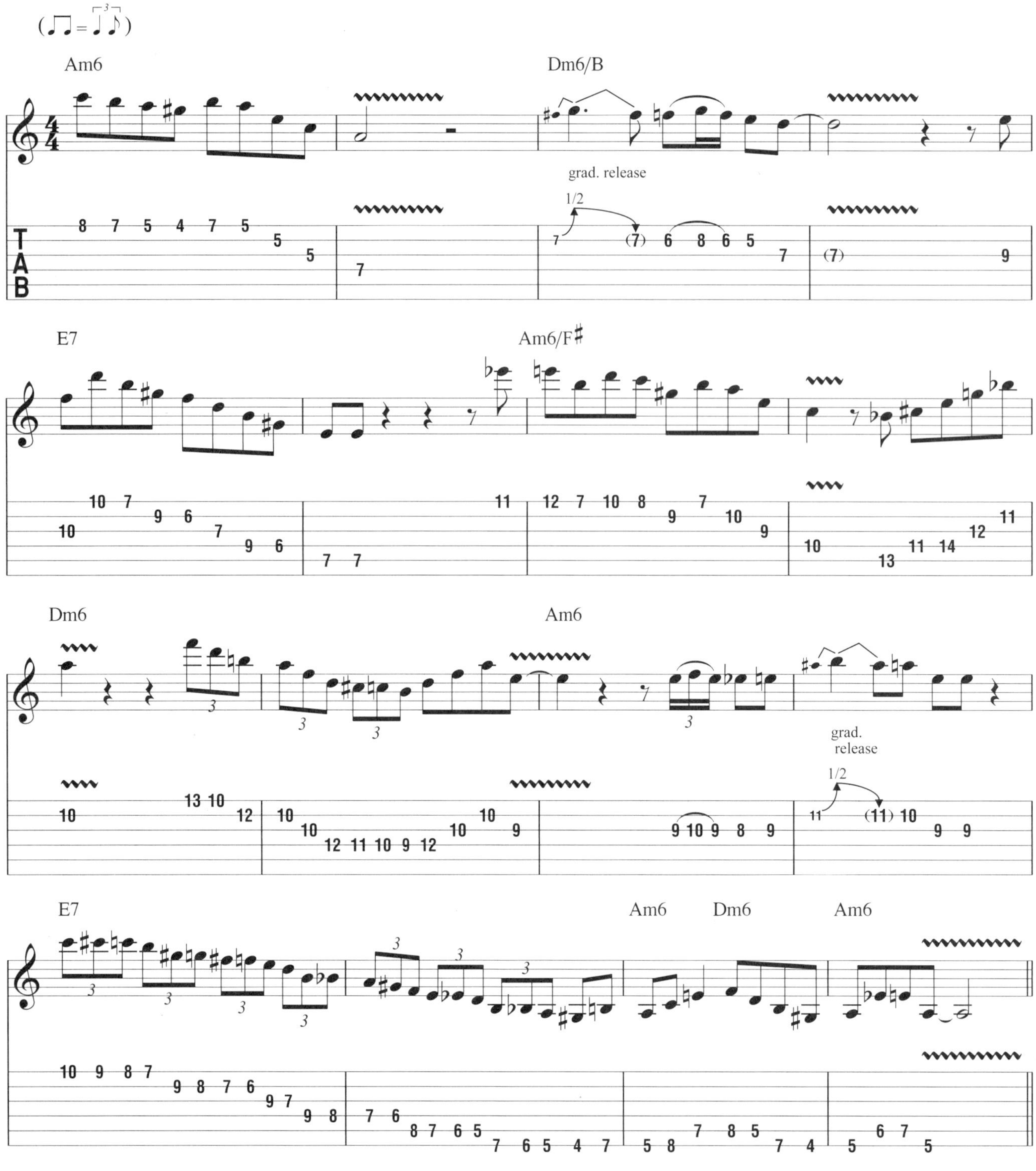

Am6
Dm6/B
grad. release
1/2
E7
Am6/F♯
Dm6
Am6
grad. release
1/2
E7
Am6
Dm6
Am6

Solo 2

Solo 2 is based on the changes to "Dark Eyes."

Chords Used

A7
5fr
1 2 4 3
Dm
5fr
1 3 4 2 1
B♭6
5fr
2 1 4 3
Gm6
2 1 3 3
Gm6/E
7fr
1 3 2 4
E°7
6fr
2 3 1 4
C♯°7
2 3 1 4

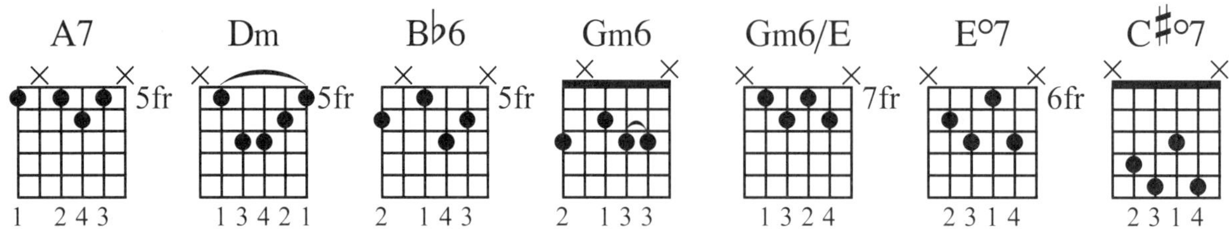

Rhythm

Again, we use the alternate minor 6 voicing in measures 9, 10, and 15. Note the E°7 and C♯°7 chords used in measures 13 and 14. I'm using these chords as substitutions for the A7 chord. They both function as A7♭9 voicings.

Solo Breakdown

- Measures 1 and 2: A common altered chord lick that incorporates the ♯9 and ♭9.
- Measures 3 and 4: A simple Dm6 arpeggio.
- Measures 5 and 6: Very similar to measures 1 and 2, but I start with a slide that suggests a chromatic run. Notice how these two phrases have a similar rhythmic motif. This gives measures 1–8 cohesion by creating a call and answer theme.
- Measures 7 and 8: A B♭ major lick.
- Measures 9 and 10: I use a tremolo effect on the Gm6 chord to grab attention.
- Measures 11 and 12: A Dm6 arpeggio lick.
- Measures 13 and 14: I use one of Django's signature sweep licks to play a diminished arpeggio.
- Measures 15 and 16: A standard ending, similar to the one used in the "Minor Swing" solo but descending this time.

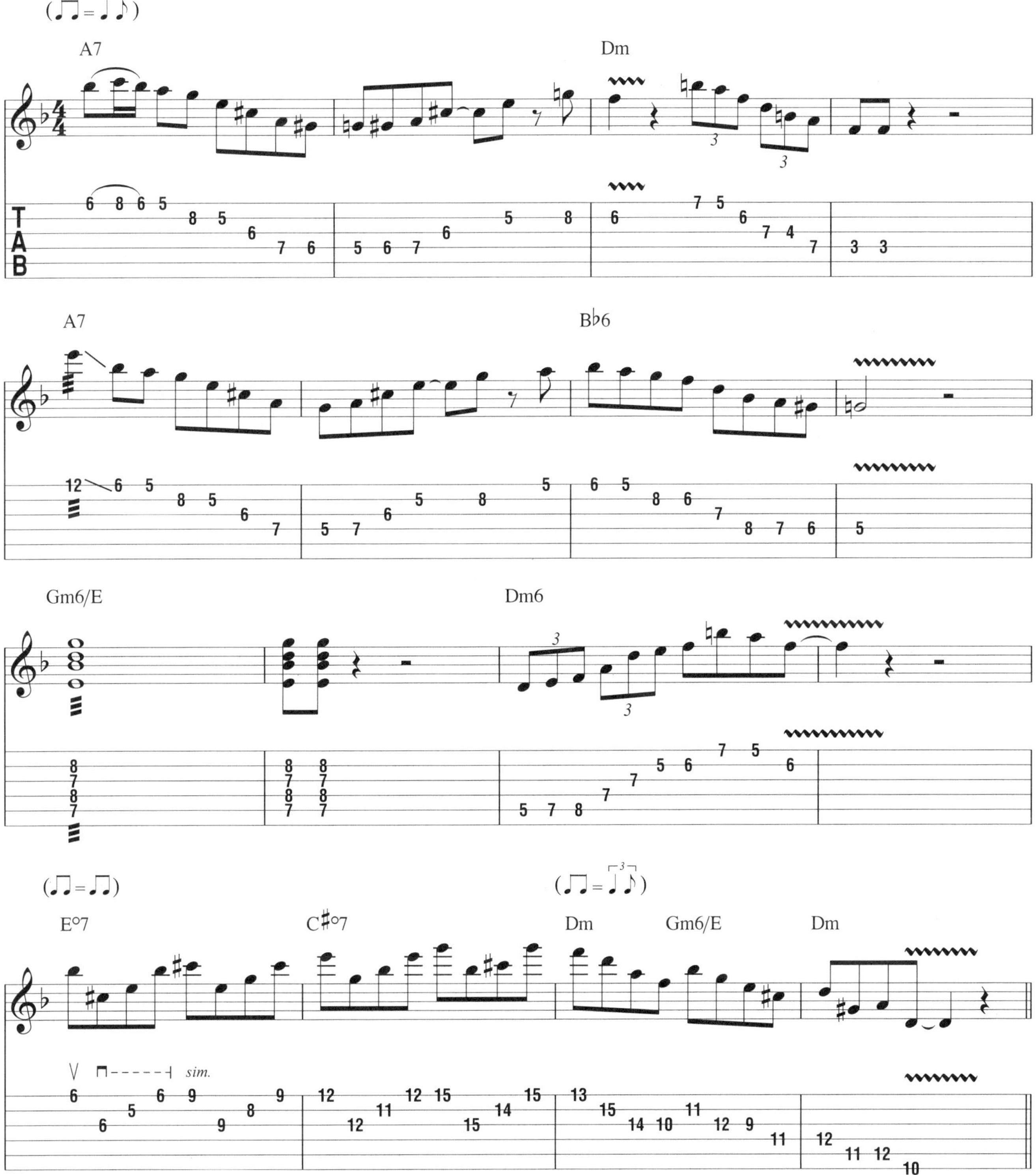

Solo 3

Solo 3 is based on the changes to "Bossa Dorado."

Chords Used

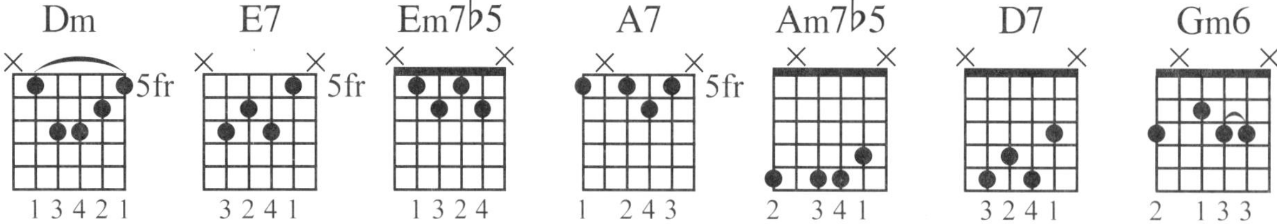

Rhythm

For this tune, we'll use the Gypsy bossa rhythm. Note that in measure 5 we are using the same alternate minor 6 chord voicing we used in the previous examples, but this time it's functioning as an Em7♭5 chord.

Solo

- Measures 1 and 2: A simple Dm arpeggio using an approach note before each chord tone.
- Measures 3 and 4: An E7 arpeggio with a chromatic lead-in starting at the end of measure 2.
- Measures 5 and 6: I play a Gm6 arpeggio over the Em7♭5 and an altered lick over the A7 that incorporates the ♭9 and ♯9.
- Measures 7 and 8: A simple hammer-on/pull-off enclosure.
- Measures 9 and 10: I play a Cm6 arpeggio over the Am7♭5 and an enclosure over the D7.
- Measures 11 and 12: I repeat the enclosure lick but adapt it to fit over the Gm6. I follow up with another typical Django bend (♭5 to 5).
- Measures 13 and 14: I again treat the Em7♭5 chord as a Gm6 chord. Over the A7, I play the same pattern but three frets higher, essentially a Bm6 arpeggio. This gives the A7 chord an altered sound by emphasizing the ♭9, ♯9, and ♯5.
- Measures 15 and 16: A standard Hot Club ending.

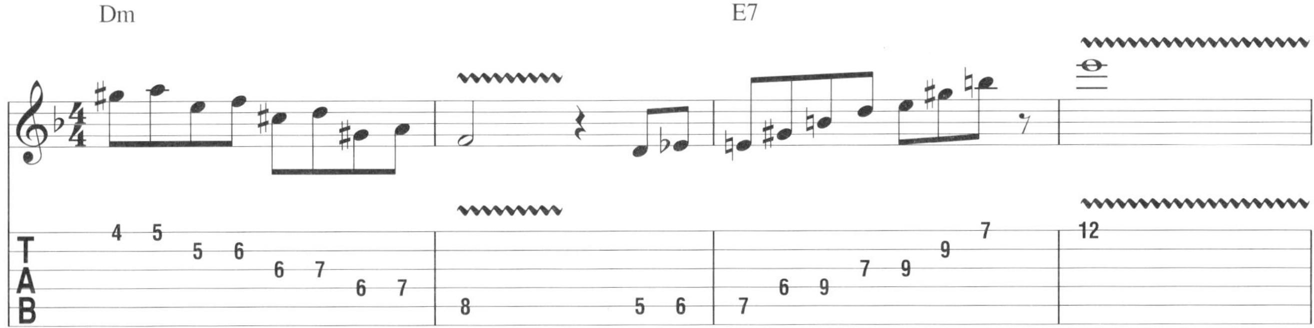
Dm
E7
T
A
B

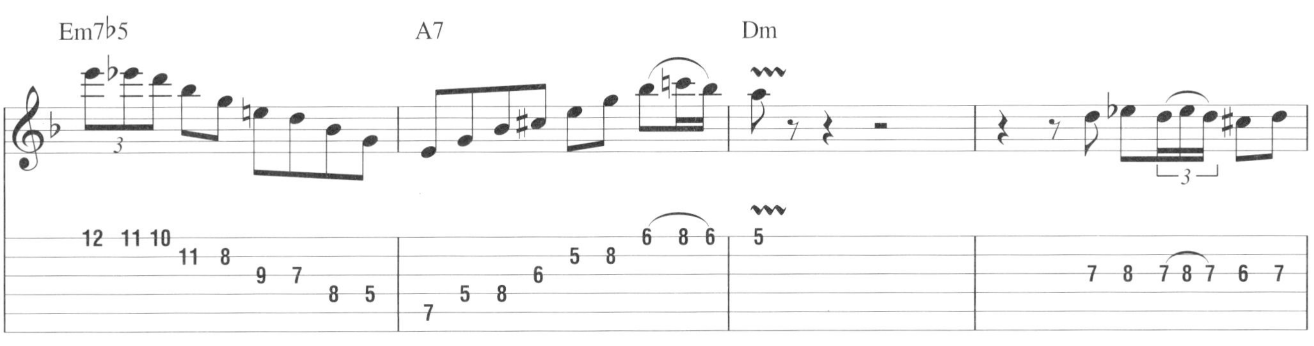
Em7♭5
A7
Dm

Am7♭5
D7
Gm6
grad. release
1/2

Em7♭5
A7
Dm6

Solo 4

Solo 4 is based on the changes to "Troublant Bolero."

Chords Used

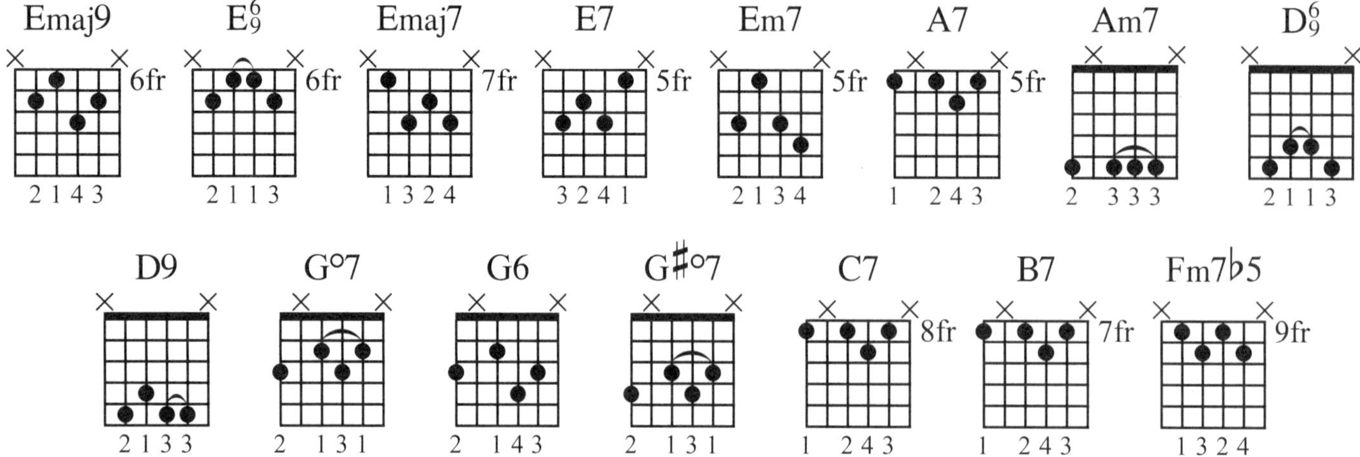

Rhythm

In this tune, we'll use the Gypsy bolero rhythm. Note the Emaj7(9) chord. This is usually preferred over a straight maj7 chord. Also note the F♯m7♭5 chord in measure 13. What minor 6 chord could you use as a substitution for this?

Solo Breakdown

- Measures 1 and 2: An Emaj7 arpeggio played in triplets. Since the arpeggio contains four notes, the triplet figure accentuates a different note each time, creating an interesting rhythmic effect.
- Measures 3 and 4: I maintain the triplet pattern but extend it by a few notes so as not to finish predictably on the first beat.
- Measures 5 and 6: I sweep through the D chord and then play the basic arpeggio of the C and B triads.
- Measures 6 and 8: Over the E6/9 chord, I just hit a couple chord tones before launching into an E7♭9 arpeggio over the E7.
- Measures 9 and 10: I use a hammer-on/pull-off enclosure lick on the Am7. I use the same lick over the D7, just shifting it up three frets so it fits the chord tones.
- Measures 11 and 12: The G° and G6 go by quickly, so I'm just hitting chord tones. Over the G♯°, I play the arpeggio. Notice the symmetrical pattern.
- Measures 13 and 14: I just hang on a couple notes before launching into the 16th-note run over the B7. Here, I play an Am6 arpeggio. This has an interesting, altered sound that emphasizes the ♭9 and ♭5 of the B7 chord.
- Measures 15 and 16: I play an E arpeggio with approach notes and finish with the natural harmonics of the B and E strings.

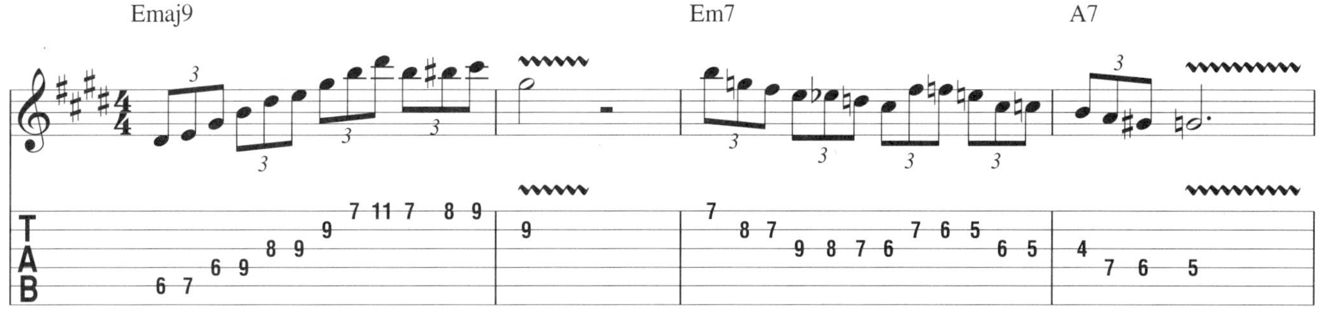
Emaj9
Em7
A7

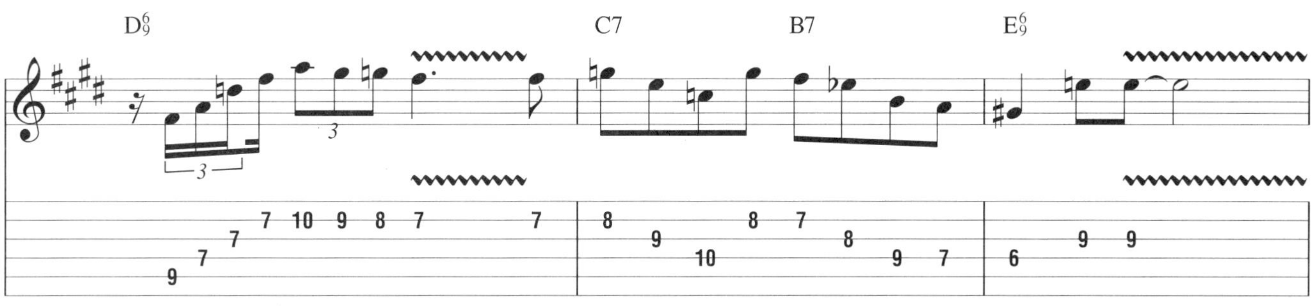
D6/9
C7
B7
E6/9

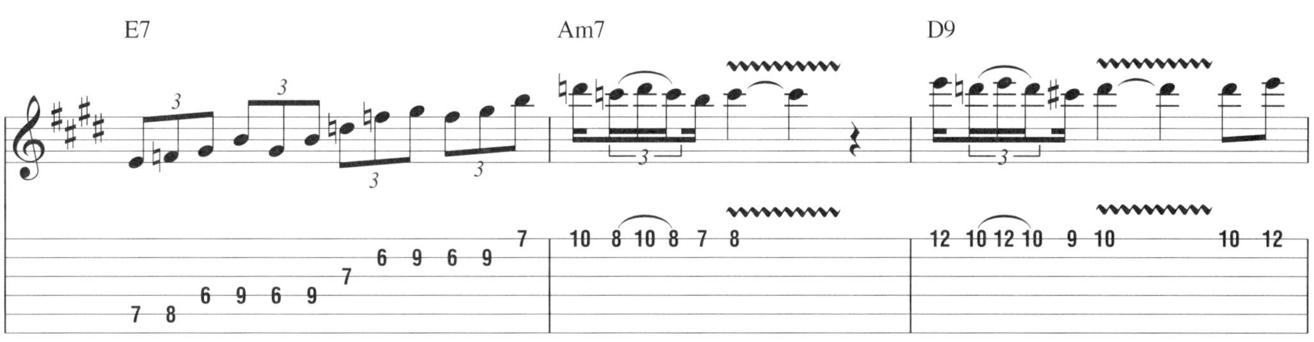
E7
Am7
D9

G°7
G6
G♯°7
F♯m7♭5

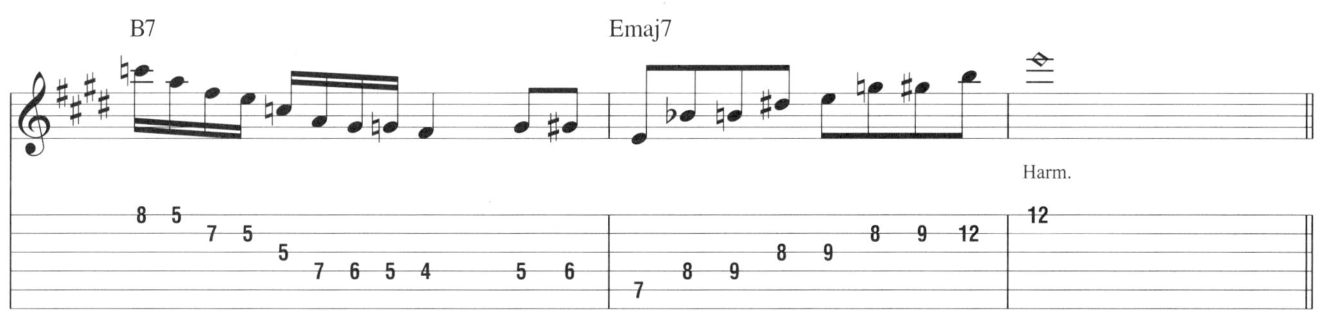
B7
Emaj7
Harm.

Solo 5

Solo 5 is based on "Rhythm Changes."

Chords Used

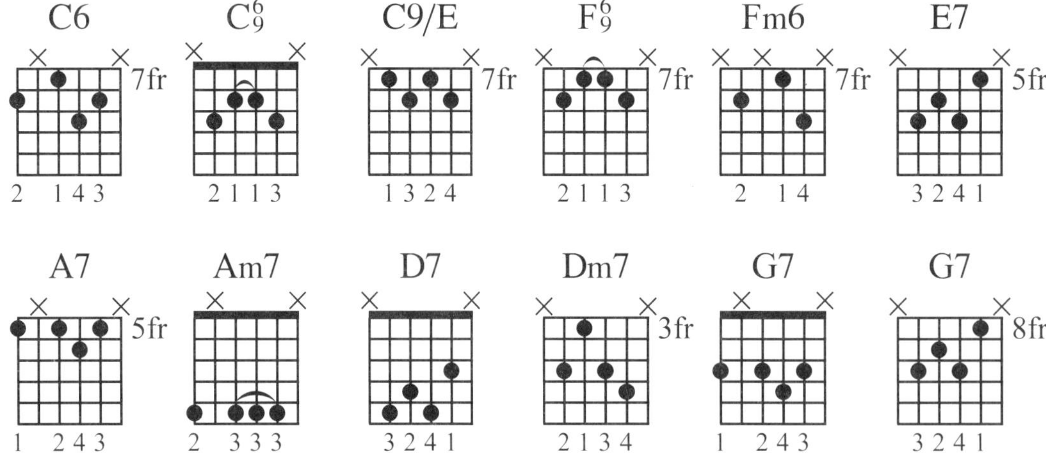

"Rhythm Changes" refers to the George Gershwin song "I Got Rhythm" that became a template for dozens of songs in the jazz repertoire. Some of Django's most popular tunes are based on "Rhythm Changes": "Belleville," "Daphne," and "Swing 42," for example. I initially found these tunes hard to solo on. The chords go by too fast in the A section to think of each one separately, and just playing around the C major scale sounded really bland. One of my teachers suggested thinking of the A section as just a I chord or alternating between a I and a V7 chord. This made things a lot easier.

Rhythm

There is a myriad of possible variations for "Rhythm Changes." Here, we'll stick to the simplest form. Note that this is a truncated version with just one A section (the traditional form would be AABA).

Solo Breakdown

- Measures 1 and 2: I just think "C" and play one of Django's signature enclosure licks.
- Measures 3 and 4: I ignore the Am7 and Dm7 and treat these two measures as a I chord and a V chord. I start with a C lick and then play a G7♭9 lick.
- Measures 5 and 6: There is a lot of harmonic movement in the accompaniment here. To contrast that, I stay on one note embellished by a slide gimmick we learned in the ornamentation section.
- Measures 7 and 8: A simple bluesy lick with a bend.
- Measures 9 and 10: An E9 arpeggio.
- Measures 11 and 12: An A9 arpeggio.
- Measures 13 and 14: A D9/13 arpeggio. Notice how I use the same rhythmic motif and finish each phrase on the same note in these four measures. This glues the passage together.
- Measures 15 and 16: I initiate the ending with a simple octave phrase.

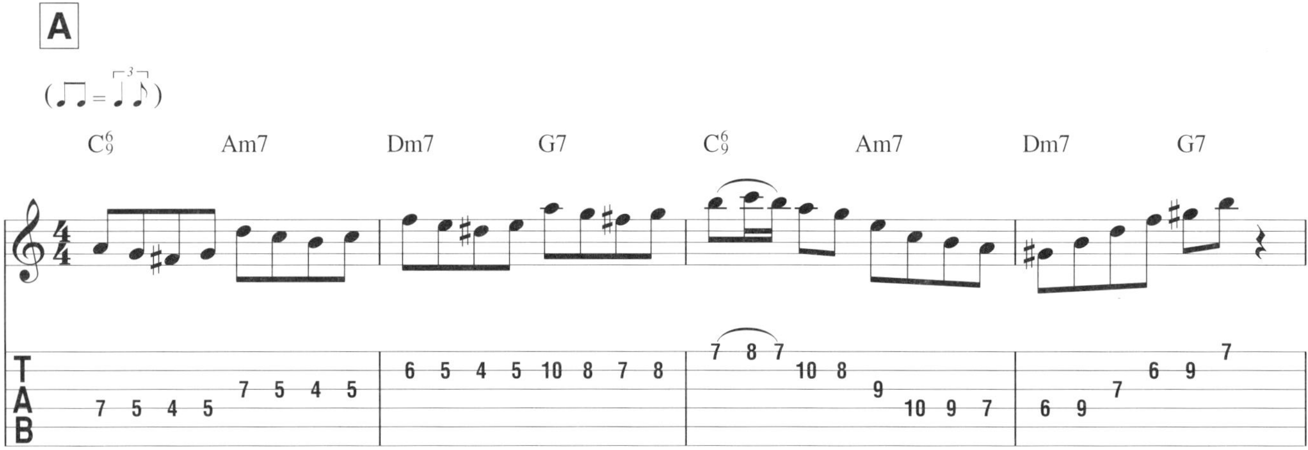

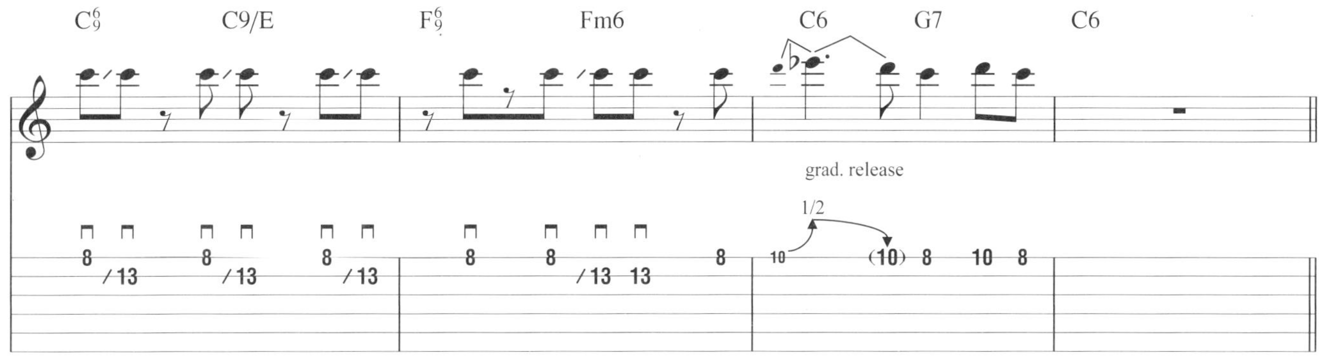

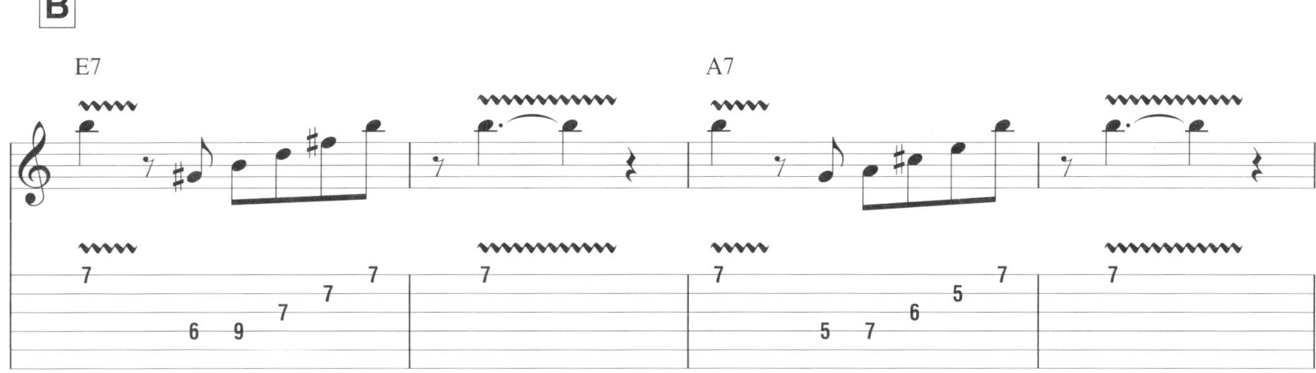

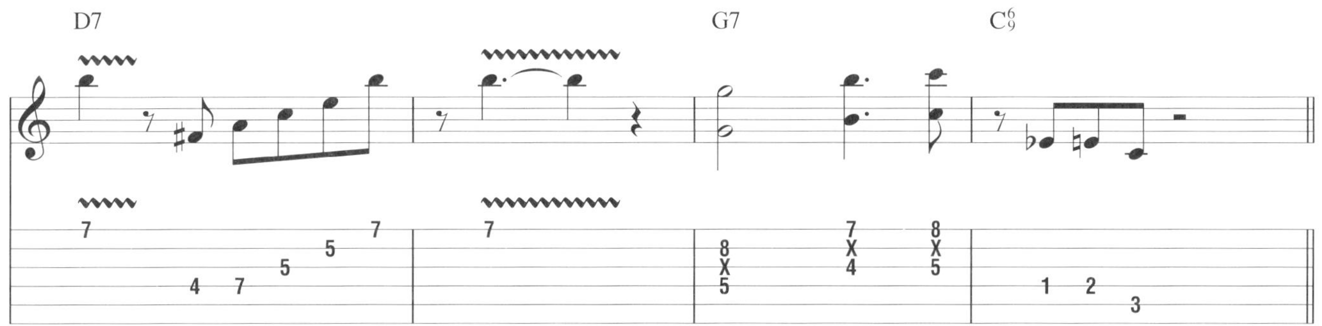

Solo 6

Solo 6 is based on a Gypsy jazz waltz.

Chords Used

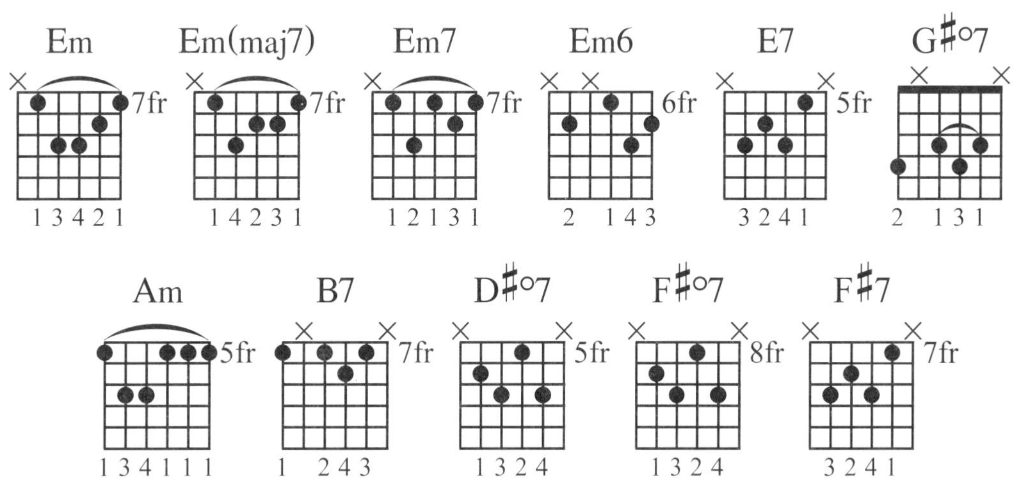

This isn't a solo per se, but it's an example of a melody you'd find in a typical Gypsy jazz waltz. Most are fairly similar and built on simple arpeggios. As I stated earlier in the book, these waltzes usually have a fairly long form with three different sections. Here, we'll just work with the A section.

Rhythm

These waltzes tend to stay on one chord for a long time, so we'll get a little more adventurous and use some alternate voicings. I use some diminished chords as substitutions for the B7 (D#°7 and F#°7) and E7 (G#°7). You'll remember that these diminished chords can function as dominant 7♭9 voicings. Also note the descending cadence in measures 17–20. This chromatic movement is a staple in Gypsy waltzes.

Solo Breakdown

- Measures 1–4: These first four measure are an Em arpeggio with the addition of the 2nd scale tone (F#). There are a lot of Gypsy waltzes that start with this exact melody.
- Measures 5–8: Here, I repeat the melody except for the last note that resolves to a note from the Am chord.
- Measures 9–12: A B7♭9 arpeggio with a couple chromatic passing tones.
- Measures 13–16: Here, I descend the B7♭9 arpeggio and resolve on the ♭3 of the Em chord.
- Measures 17–20: I restate the original melody.
- Measures 21–24: I descend an E7♭9 arpeggio that segues into an Am arpeggio.
- Measures 25–28: I start with a B7♭9 lick using some chromatic passing tones. I echo this by using another chromatic run down the Em arpeggio.
- Measures 29–32: The F#7 and B7 go by quickly, so I simply hit a couple tones from each chord. The last two measures are a simple Em arpeggio.

B7
D♯°7
Em
3
B7

Em
Em(maj7)
Em7
Em6

E7
G♯°7
Am
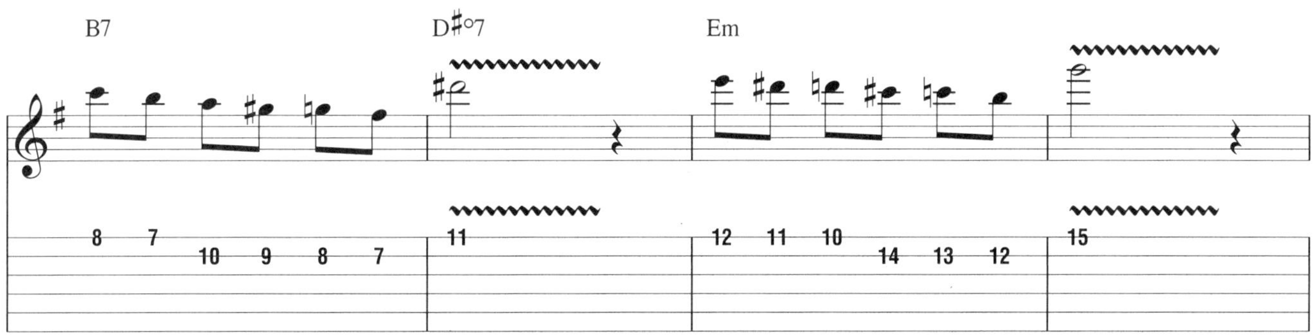
B7
D♯°7
Em
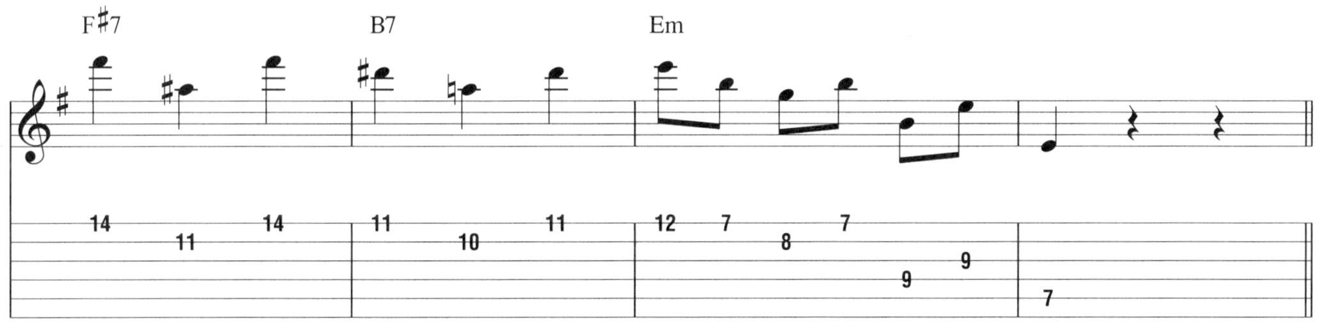
F♯7
B7
Em

Solo 7

Solo 7 is based on the changes to "Django's Castle."

Chords Used

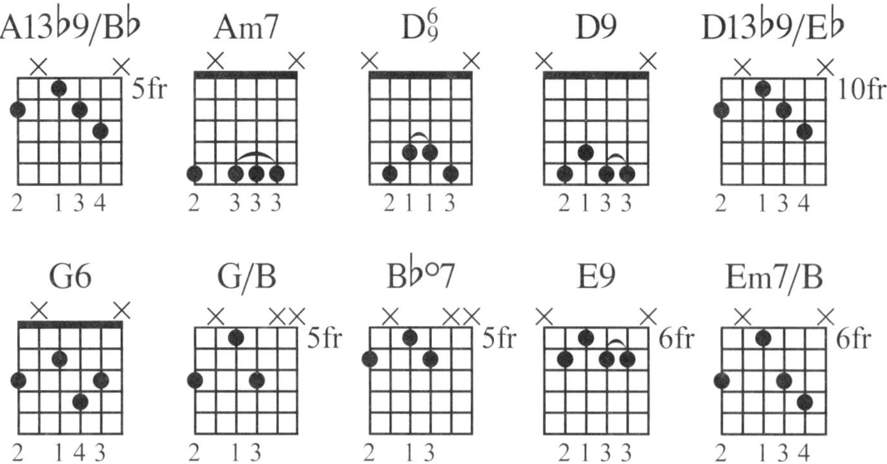

Rhythm

We'll use the "long, short" variation of La Pompe in this example. Note the use of the A13♭9/B♭ chord. This is probably the most common altered dominant chord voicing in the style. The ♭9 is actually the first note of the chord. Note also the ascending cadence in measure 9. This is often used when you have two measures of the same chord, or as a means of navigating up a 4th.

Solo Breakdown

- Measures 1 and 2: I establish a simple theme using a bend to give it a little character.
- Measures 3 and 4: I contrast this with a fast chromatic run.
- Measures 5 and 6: I return to my theme.
- Measures 7 and 8: I know the D13/E♭ is followed by a chord a 4th above, so I play an altered lick using an E♭m6/9 arpeggio. This emphasizes the ♭9, ♯5, and ♯9 of the D7 chord.
- Measures 9 and 10: I echo my original theme.
- Measures 11 and 12: I feel something fast is needed again to grab attention, so I play a single note tremolo.
- Measures 13 and 14: I play an E9 arpeggio but finish on the ♯11. This ♯11 sound is often heard on dominant 7th chords that aren't moving to a chord a 4th above. It provides a little tension before the final ii–V–I ending.
- Measures 15 and 16: I play a simple Em arpeggio and then an A7 altered phrase that contains the ♭9 and the ♭5. I bring the solo to a close by approaching the D6/9 chord chromatically from two frets below.

A13/B♭
D6/9
A13/B♭
D6/9
A13/B♭
D6/9
A13/B♭
1/2
1/2

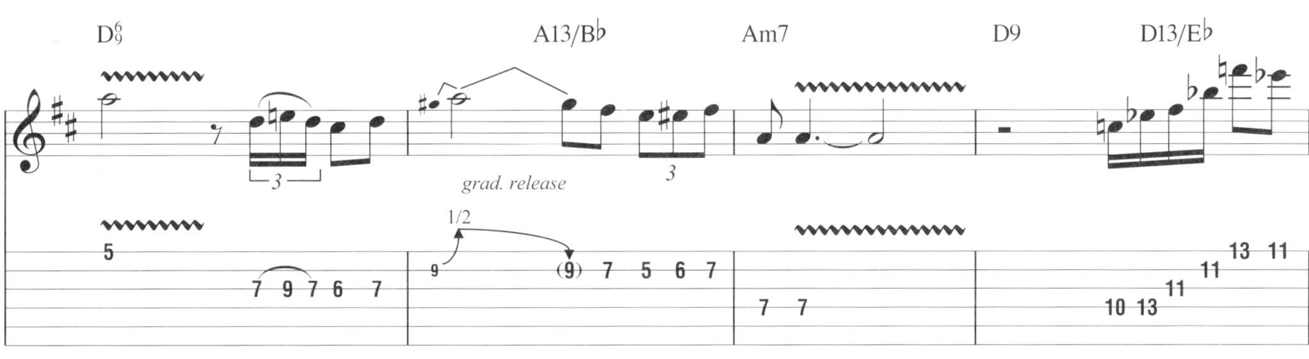
D6/9
A13/B♭
Am7
D9
D13/E♭
grad. release
1/2

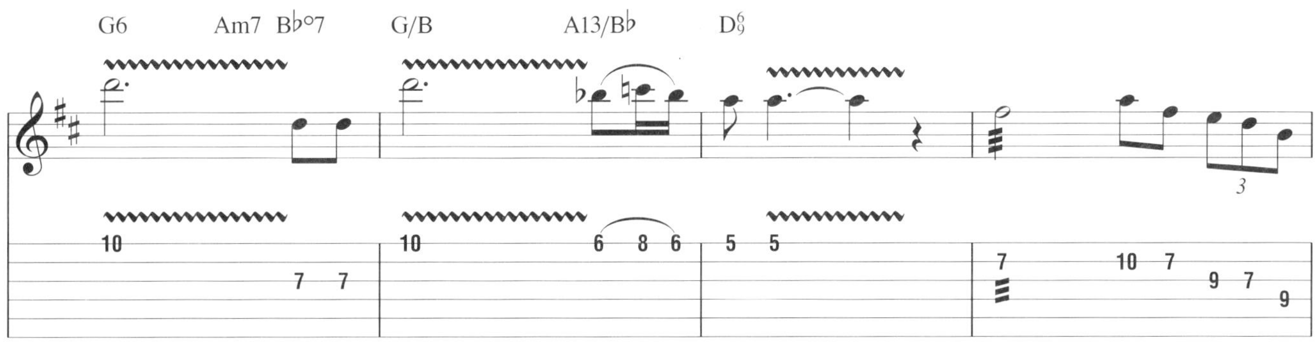
G6
Am7
B♭°7
G/B
A13/B♭
D6/9

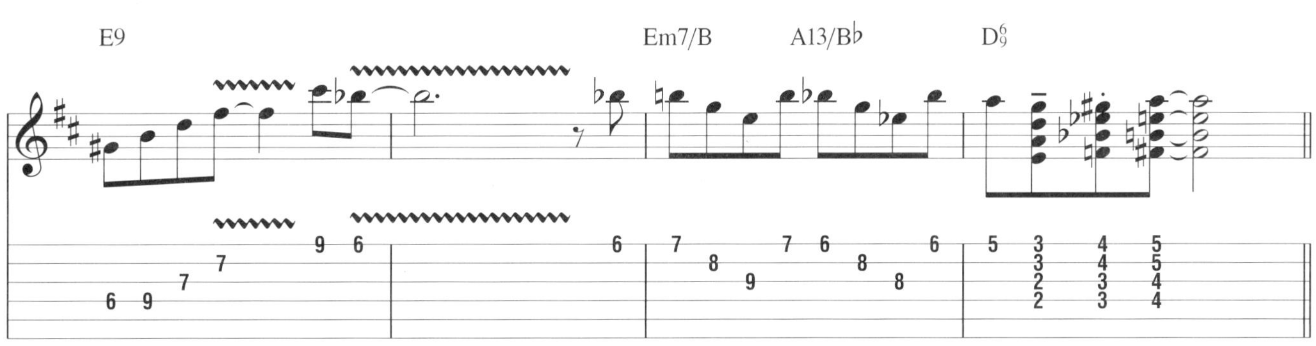
E9
Em7/B
A13/B♭
D6/9

Solo 8

Solo 8 is based on the changes to "Clair De Lune" by Joseph Kosma.

Chords Used

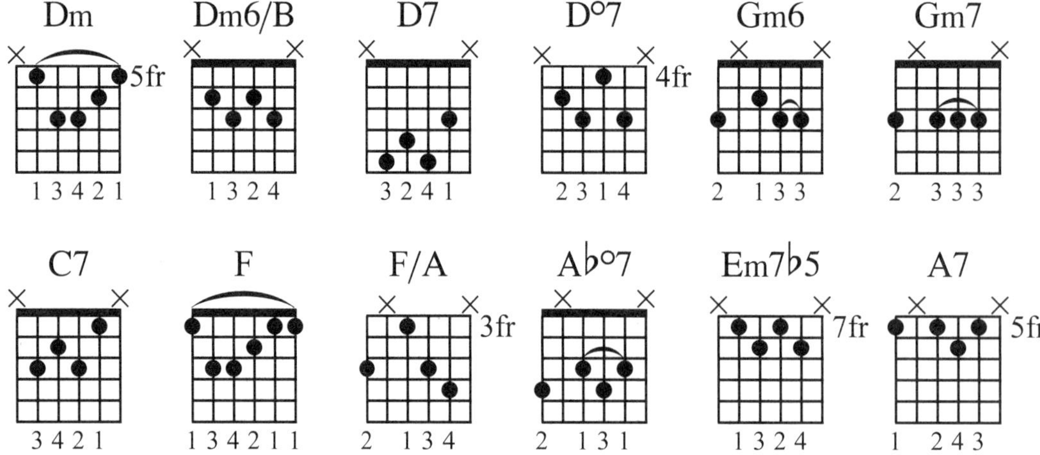

Rhythm

We'll use the "long, long" variation of La Pompe in this example with no upstroke. Note the ascending cadence in measure 4. This should look familiar. Also note the use of the Em7♭5 chord and Dm6/B chord. The multiple identities of this voicing should be starting to become familiar as well.

Solo Breakdown

- Measures 1 and 2: I lead into measure one with a sweep of a Dm arpeggio, then play a descending chromatic run that resolves on the major 3rd to emphasize the D7 chord.
- Measures 3 and 4: I repeat this motif but adapt it to fit over the Gm7 and C7 chords.
- Measures 5 and 6: Here, I am playing the same lick in both measures. Remember how the minor7♭5 and minor 6 chords are related?
- Measures 7 and 8: To contrast all the 16th notes that came before, I play some chords with tremolo.
- Measures 9–12: The signature Django sweep lick. Make sure you understand how all the voicings fit.
- Measures 13–16: In the last four measures, I am essentially winding down and just outlining each chord. Notice how the last four notes of measure 16 echo the last four of measure 14.

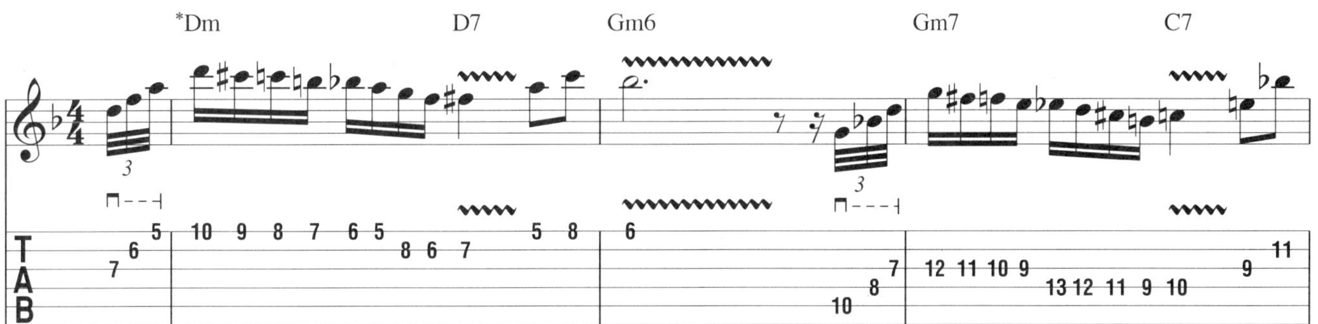

*Chord symbols reflect overall harmony.

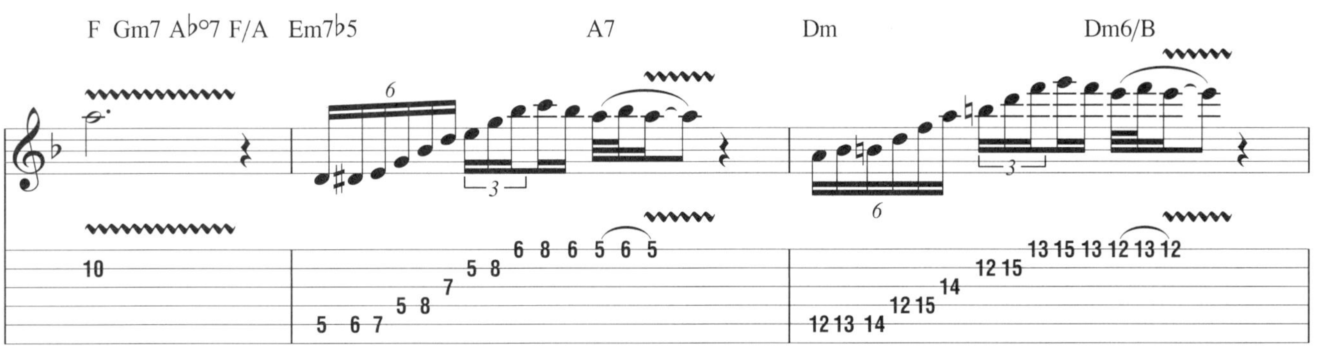

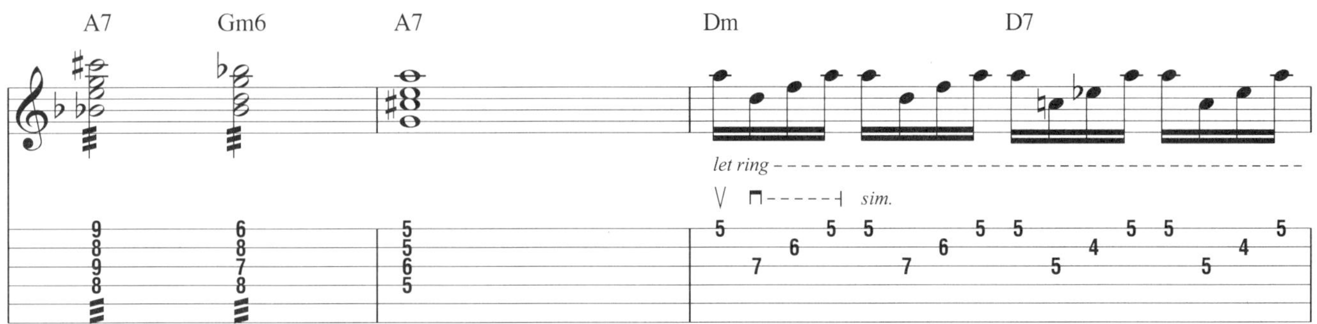

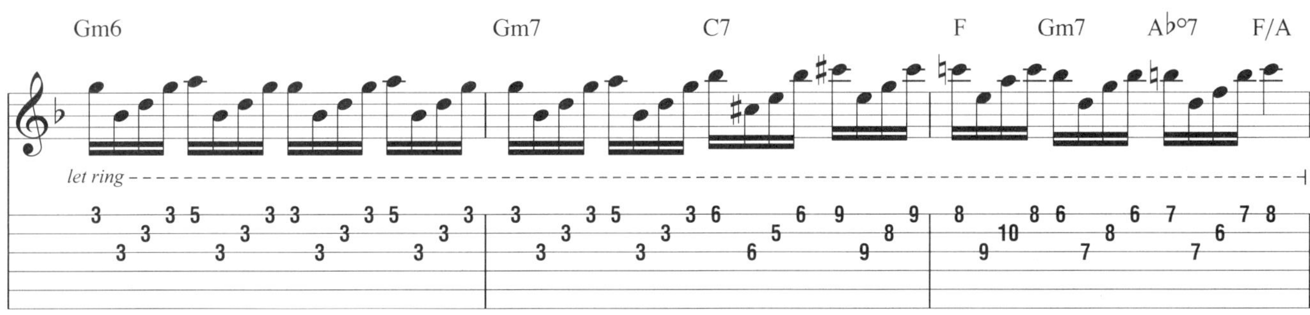

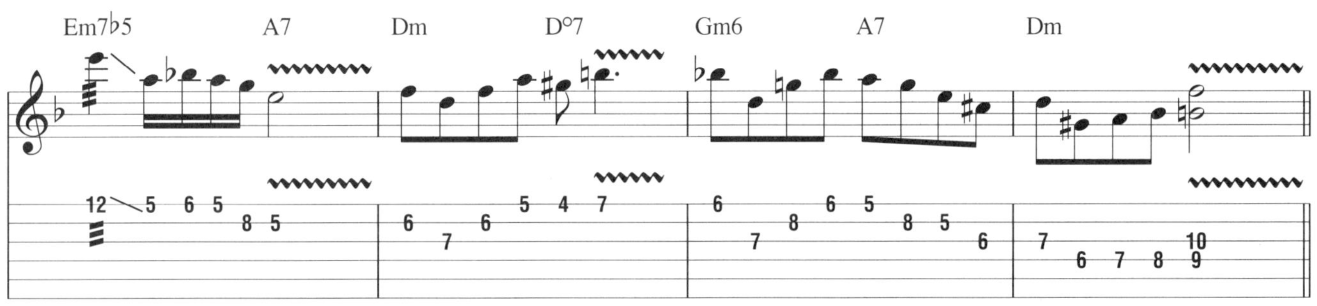

Solo 9

Solo 9 is over a 12-bar blues form.

Chords Used

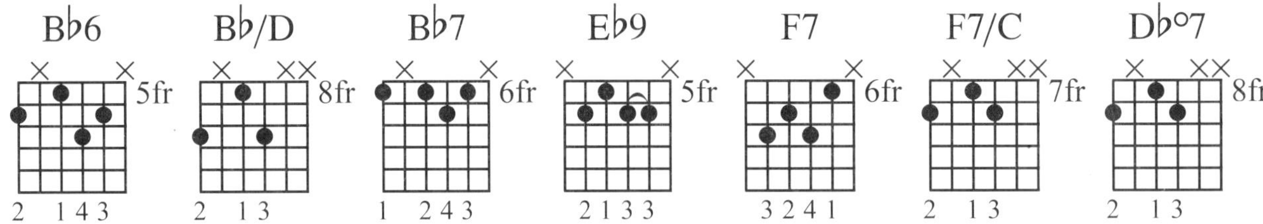

A blues played in the Gypsy style reflects those that were played by the early jazz bands in the '20s and '30s. They use more major chords, as opposed to all dominant chords, and are much less reliant on the minor pentatonic scale. In addition, they repeat the V chord in measures 9 and 10 as opposed to the V–IV changes typically used today preceding measures 11 and 12 of the turnaround. As I wanted to demonstrate the importance of using space in this solo, we'll go through the form twice.

Rhythm

The chords here are pretty straightforward. Note the descending cadence in measure 8. This is a common way to get from a I chord to a V chord and is used in lots of songs.

Solo Breakdown

- Measures 1 and 2: A simple major scale lick.
- Measures 3 and 4: I contrast this with a busier, dominant-9th phrase.
- Measures 5 and 6: Over the E♭9, I play one of our oft-seen multipurpose licks. It resolves to the 5th of the B♭ chord.
- Measures 7 and 8: A B♭maj7 arpeggio. I use a little chromatic movement at the end to resolve to the 3rd of the upcoming F9 chord.
- Measures 9 and 10: Another simple B♭ lick.
- Measures 11 and 12: I feel a little tension is needed to balance, so I play an altered lick. You could analyze this as an F7 altered phrase that uses the ♭5, ♭9, and ♯9, but it's much easier to see it as B6. This is a great trick: just arpeggiate the chord one half step above the I chord to get an a V7 altered sound.
- Measures 13–16: I want to raise the intensity, so I switch to chords that I attack from a half step below. We've used this shape as a m6 and m7♭5 voicing. Here, it functions as a dominant 9 chord.
- Measures 17 and 18: I resume single-note phrases with a dominant-9th arpeggio lick.
- Measures 19 and 20: A bluesy major-scale lick.
- Measures 21 and 22: I'm ramping up for the ending with a long lick that descends an F9 arpeggio and then ascends an F7♭9 arpeggio.
- Measures 23 and 24: One of the standard Django endings.

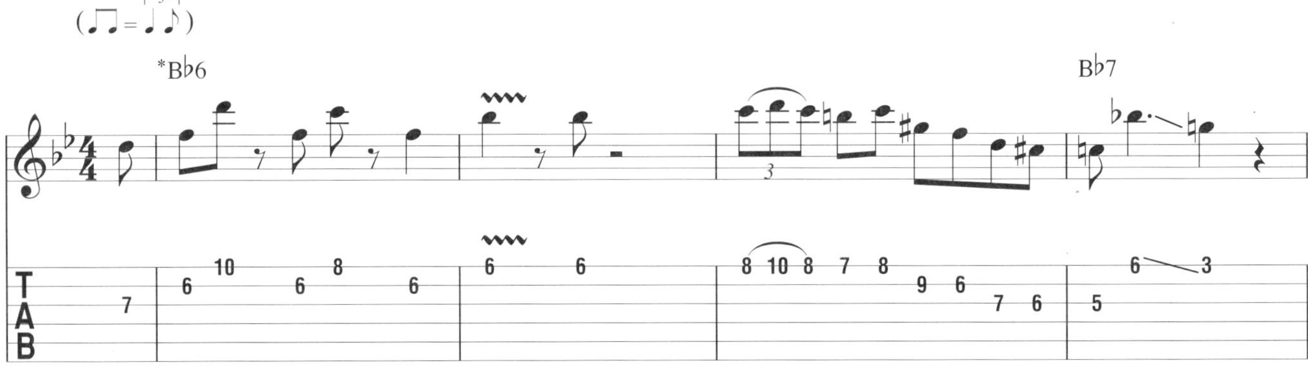

*Chord symbols reflect overall harmony.

E♭9
B♭6
B♭/D
D♭°7
F7/C
F7
B♭6
F7
B♭6
B♭7
E♭9
B♭5
B♭/D
D♭°7
F7/C
F7
B♭6

Solo 10

Solo 10 is based on the changes to "Blues En Mineur."

Chords Used

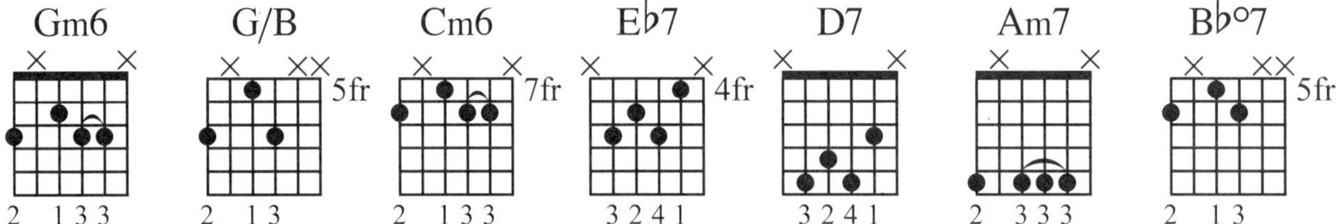

There aren't many minor blues in the Gypsy repertoire, but "Blues En Mineur" is a go-to in jam sessions. As with the major blues, you won't hear many pentatonic or blues-scale licks. The approach is much more arpeggio based.

Rhythm

The chords here, again, are pretty straightforward. It's a standard La Pompe rhythm, but it's a little crisper this time with a less pronounced up stroke. Note the ascending cadence in measure 16. We've seen this used in a major context, but it works in a minor key as well.

Solo Breakdown

- Measures 1 and 2: A simple lick using a typical Django bend from the ♭9 to the 9.
- Measures 3 and 4: I quote from another Django tune "Douce Ambiance." "Quoting" is playing a little bit of the melody from a different song. Over the Gm6 chord, I superimpose a G7♭9 lick. Notice, as before, that I don't play this lick until the second half of the measure.
- Measures 5 and 6: A quote from the actual "Blues En Mineur" melody.
- Measures 7 and 8: I play a short enclosure lick that echoes the one in measure 3 before launching into a long chromatic run.
- Measures 9 and 10: I punctuate this fast with the E♭7 chord, and then I run down a D7♭9 arpeggio.
- Measures 11 and 12: We've reached the end of the first 12 measures, so I decide to introduce a new motif. I start by quoting the first three notes of Django's tune "Artillerie Lourde." I use this as a call-and-answer device in the next four measures.
- Measures 13 and 14: I respond to the first call with a tremolo chord.
- Measures 15 and 16: I respond to the second call with a Gm6 arpeggio that segues into a G7♭9 arpeggio.
- Measures 17 and 18: I continue the triplet pattern with a Cm6 arpeggio.
- Measures 19 and 20: I fall back on my favorite Gm6 arpeggio lick.
- Measures 21 and 22: To signal the end of my solo, I switch to chords.
- Measures 23 and 24: The standard Hot Club ending but using octaves.

*Chord symbols reflect overall harmony.

Cm6
Gm6

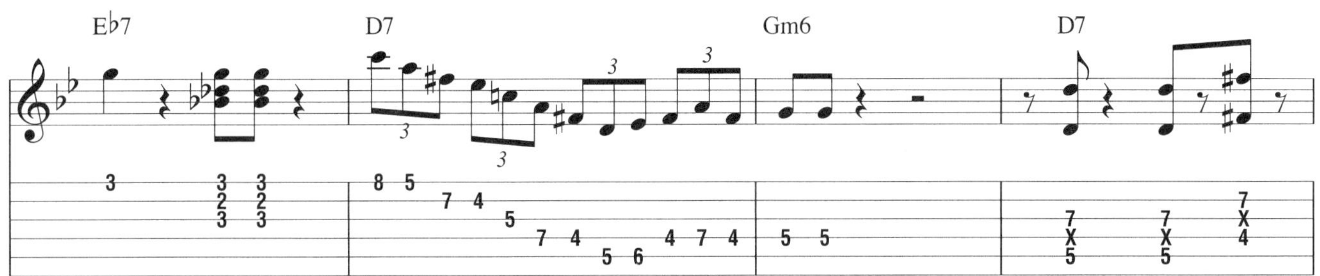
E♭7
D7
Gm6
D7

Gm6
Am7
B♭°7
G/B

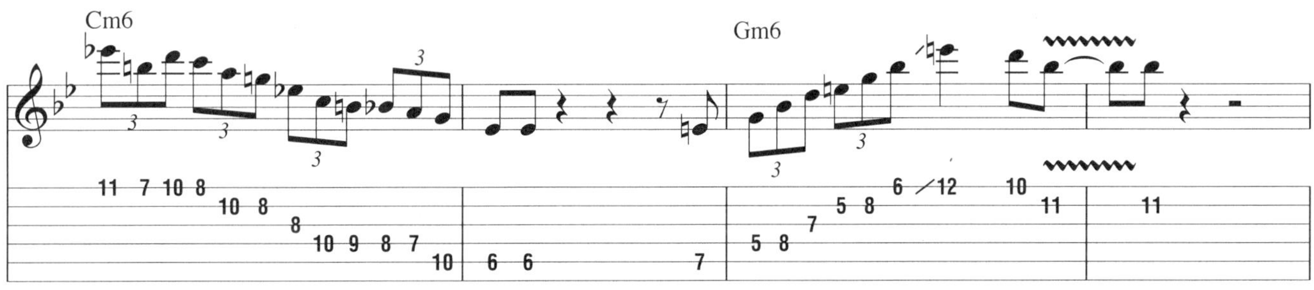
Cm6
Gm6

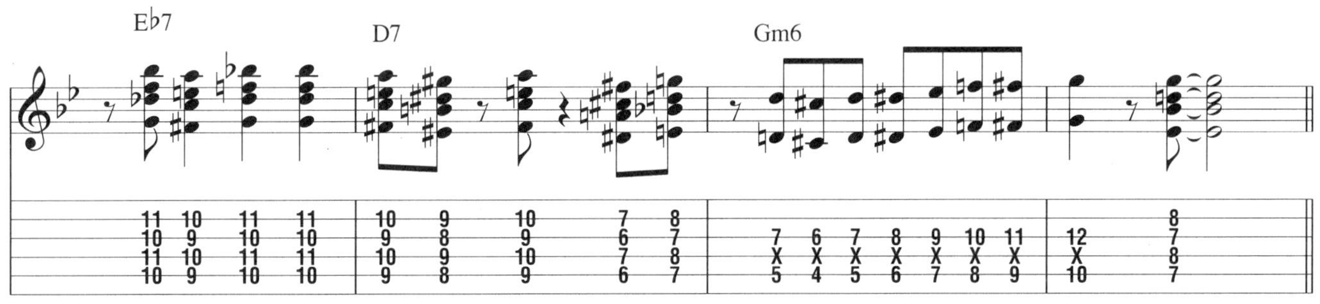
E♭7
D7
Gm6

PRACTICE TRACKS

TRACK 1

This is based on the chord changes to "Minor Swing."

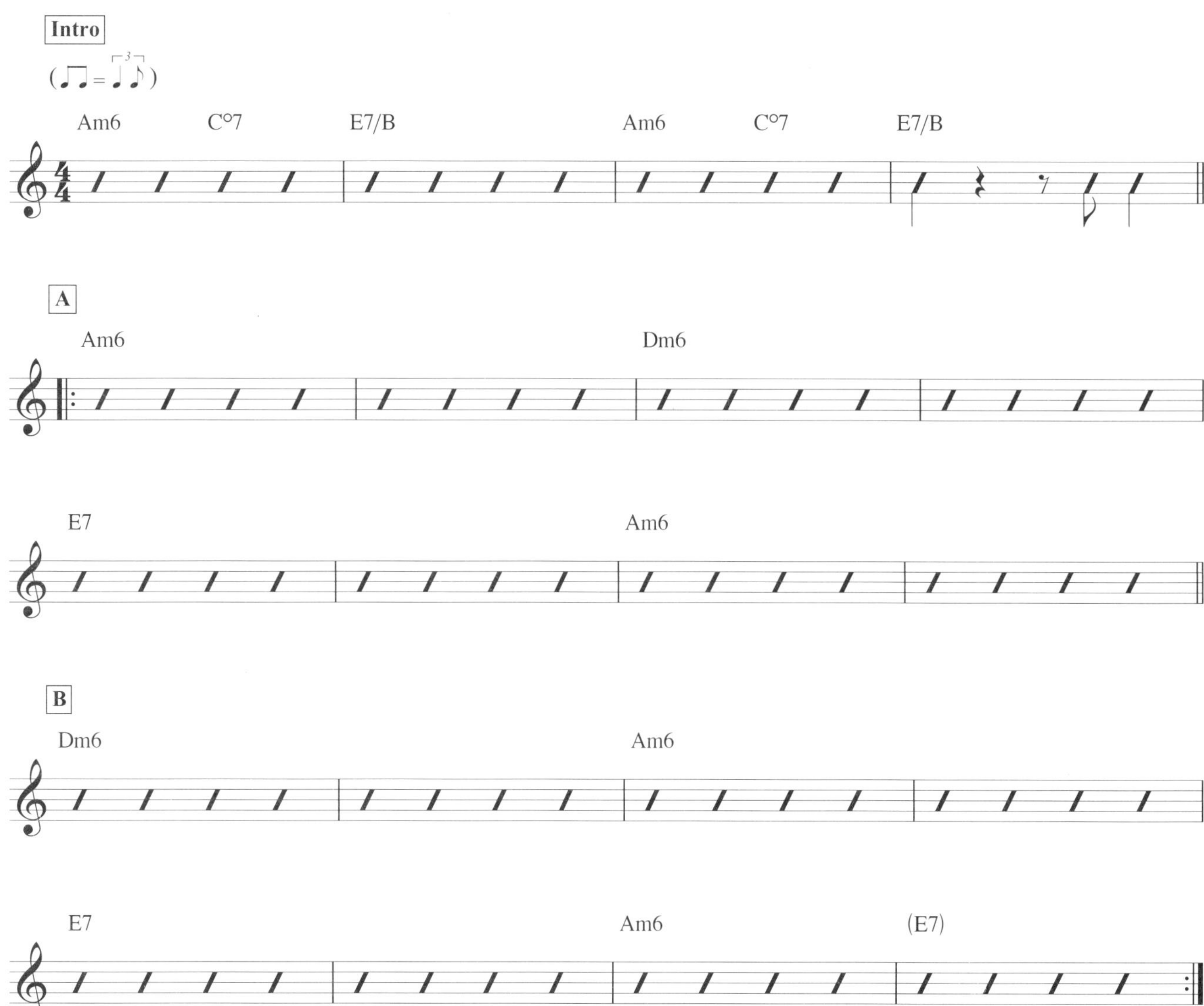

TRACK 2

This is based on the chord changes to "Dark Eyes."

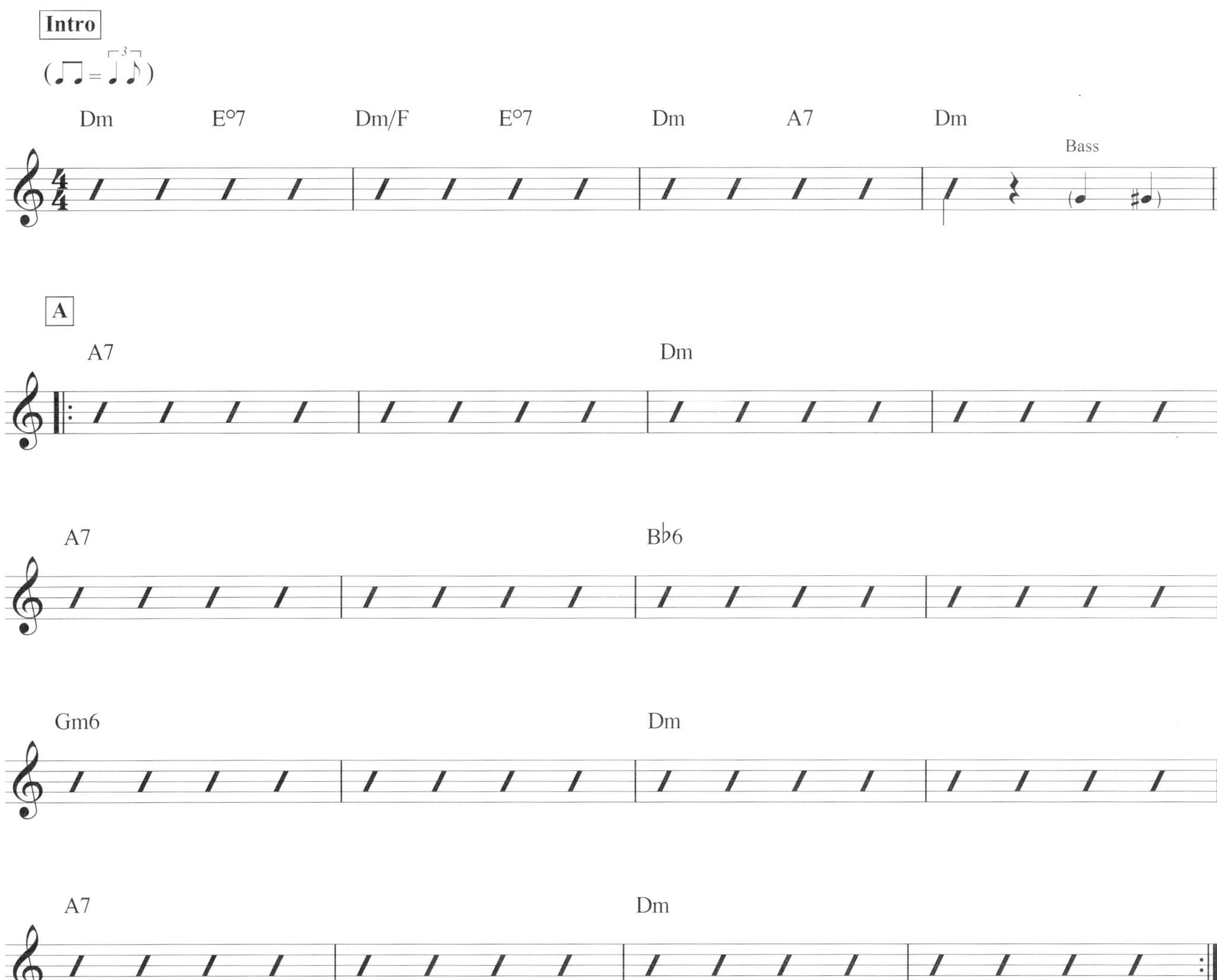

TRACK 3

This is based on the chord changes to "Bossa Dorado."

TRACK 4

This is based on the chord changes to "Troublant Bolero."

TRACK 5

This is based on "Rhythm Changes."

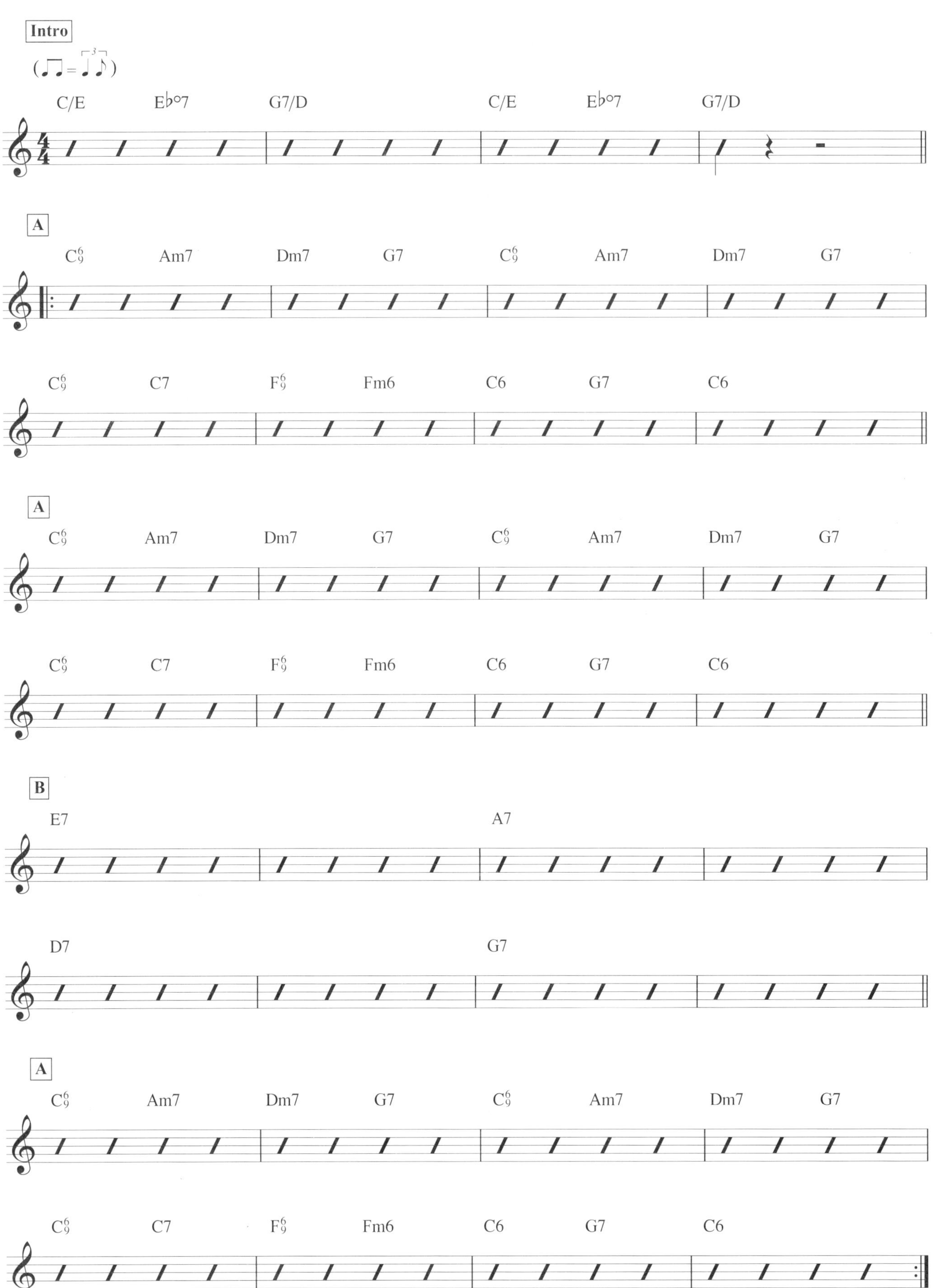

TRACK 6

This is based on a Gypsy waltz.

TRACK 7

This is based on the chord changes to "Django's Castle."

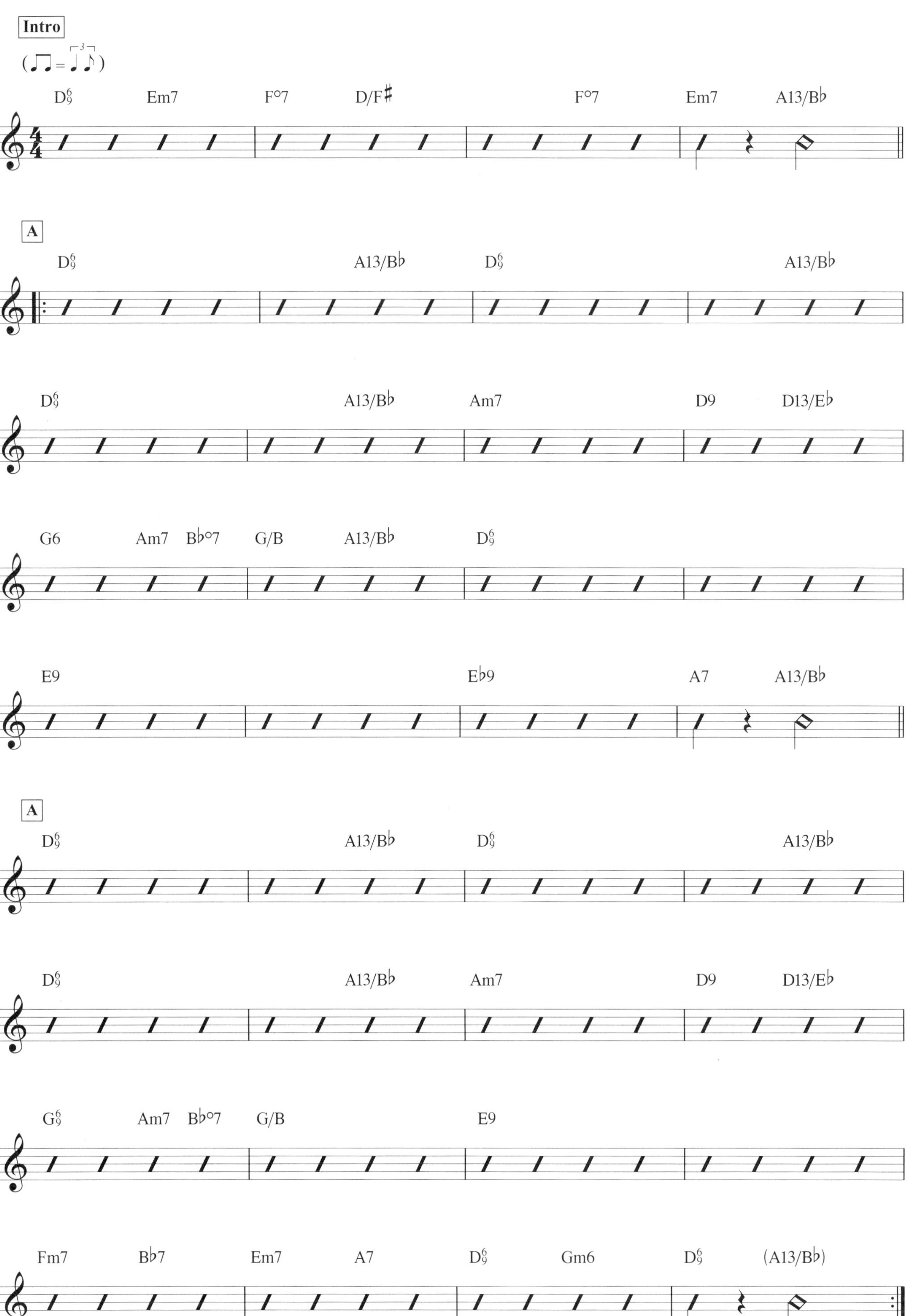

TRACK 8

This is based on the chord changes to "Clair De Lune."

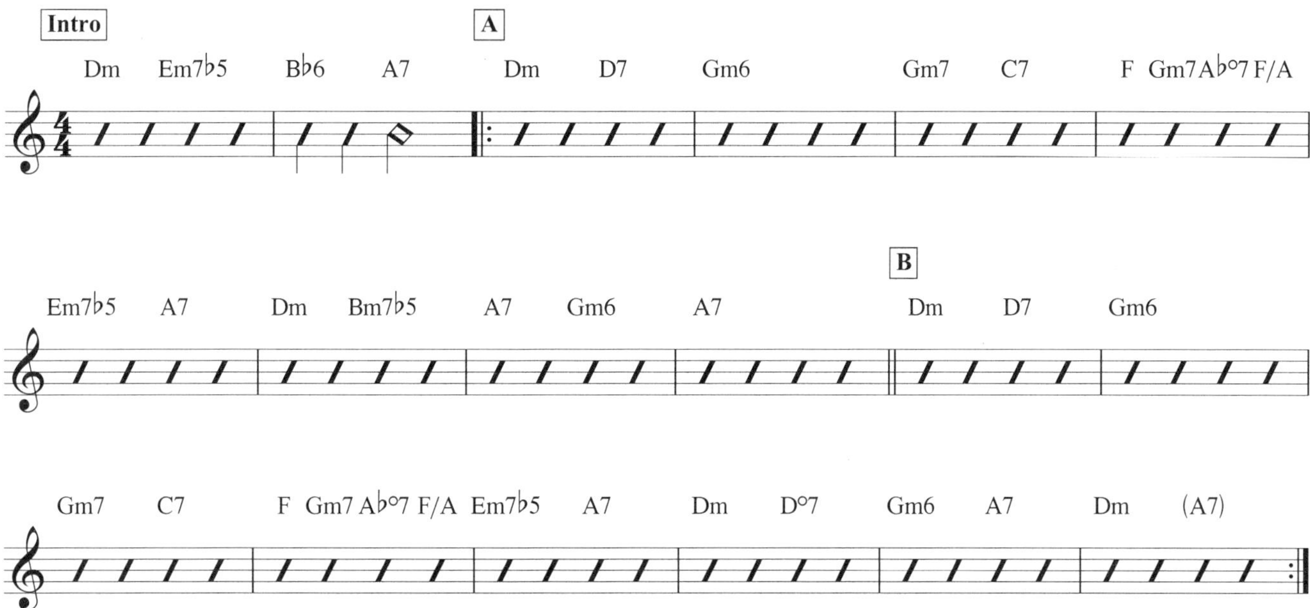

TRACK 9

This is based on a major blues.

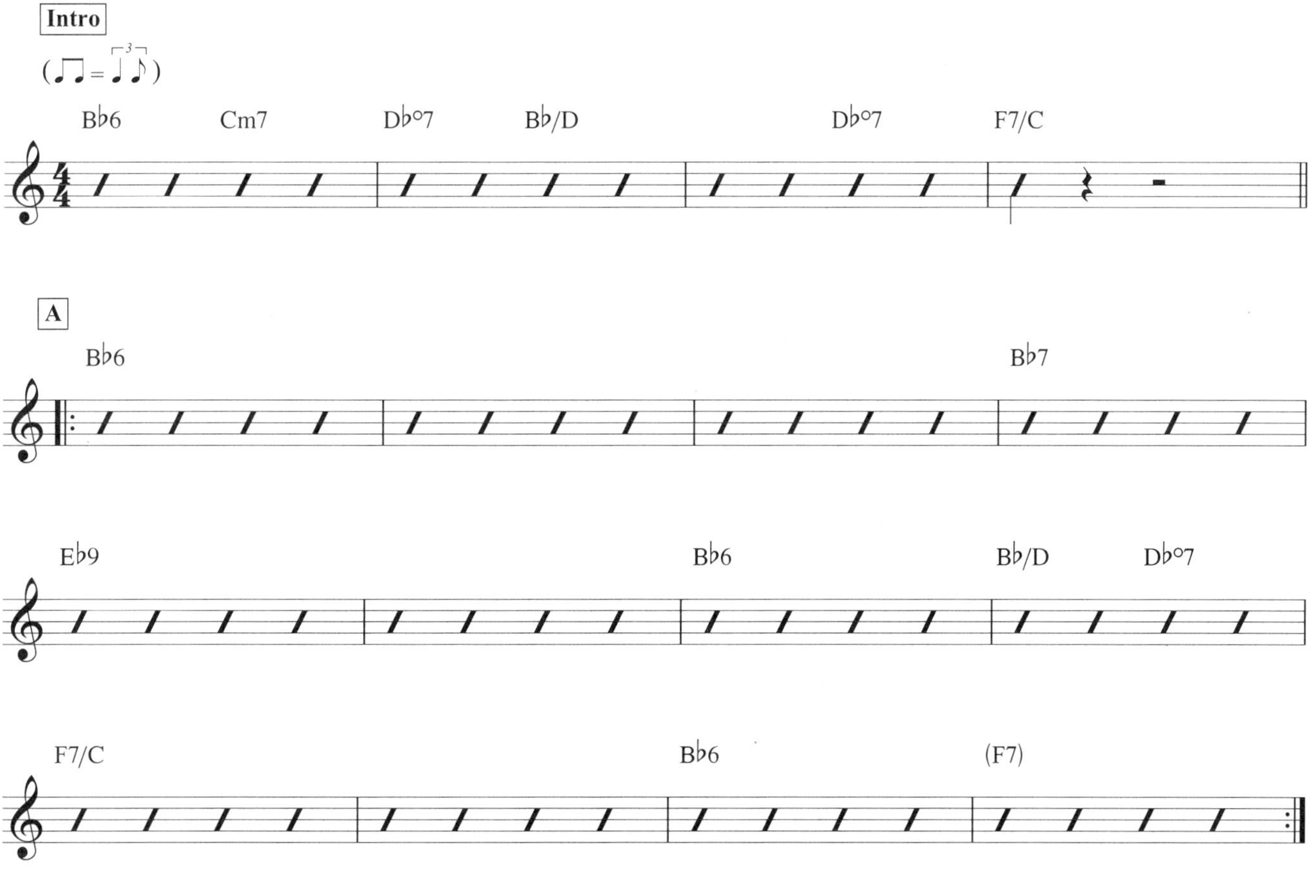

TRACK 10

This is based on a minor blues.

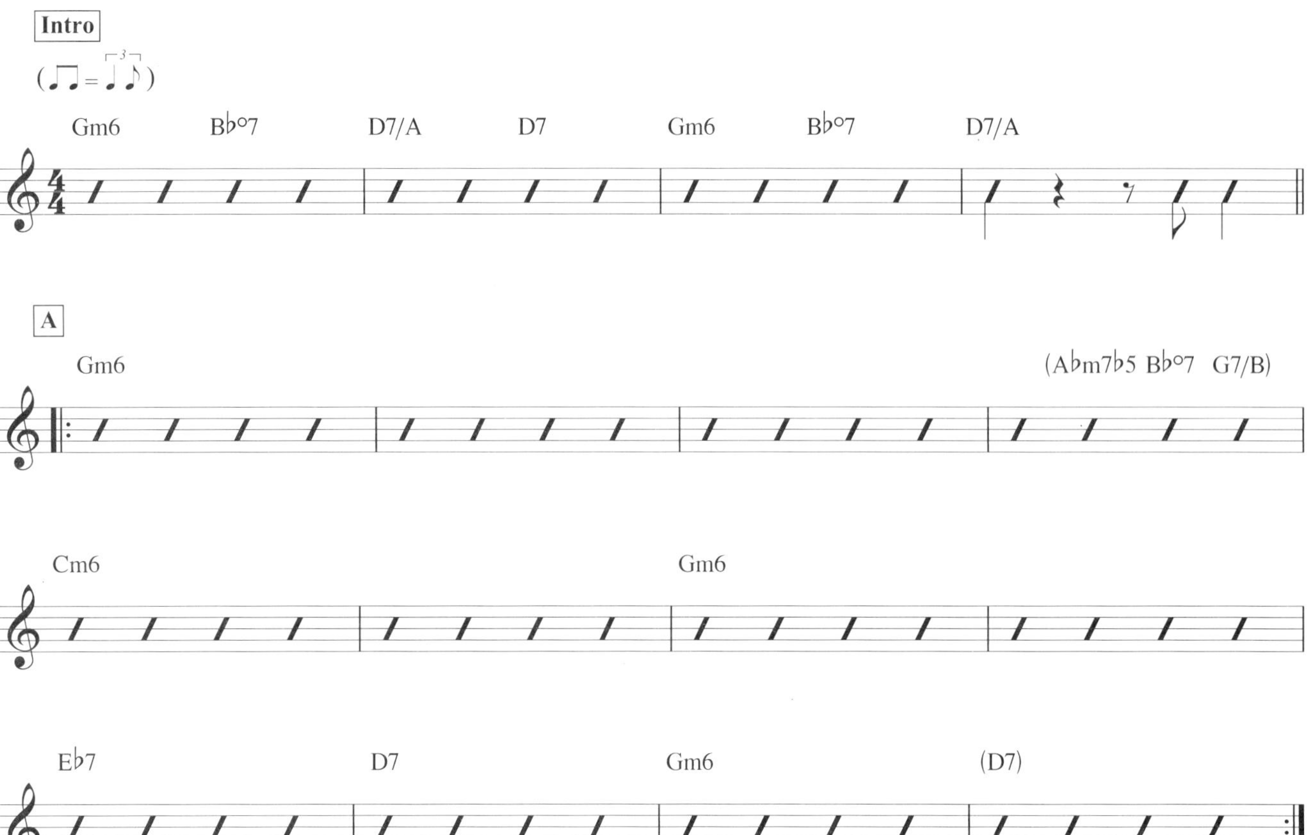

APPENDIX

Tunes You Should Know

When you take part in a jam session, it's expected that you'll lead some of the tunes. Below is a list of ten tunes commonly played at a Gypsy jam session for a start.

"Minor Swing"

"Dark Eyes"

"Honey Suckle Rose"

"Coquette"

"Swing 42"

"Djangology"

"Sweet Georgia Brown"

"Troublant Bolero"

"Nuages"

"Bossa Dorado"

Some Advice on Practicing

- Establish specific goals.

It's easy to get dispersed, especially with so much information available. Give yourself some specific short-term and long-term goals to work towards. A short-term goal might be learning a new lick or melody. A long-term goal might be memorizing ten songs. Write these goals down and keep track of your progress.

- Be consistent.

Daily practice is critical. It doesn't have to be long, but it needs to be consistent. If you practice one thing on Monday and something else on Tuesday, you're cheating yourself. Make sure you stay on task, and practice from the list of goals you've established.

- Use a metronome.

Getting my beginning students to use a metronome is like taking my cat to the vet: serious resistance. Most accomplished players will tell you, however, that the metronome is their best friend. It's always there for you, ready to play, and it never lies.

- Learn melodies.

There are lots of players who can shred over changes but too few that know the *head* (melody) to a tune. The melody is hugely important. It should be the primary inspiration for your solo. Learning melodies and analyzing how they navigate the chord changes will also improve your soloing immensely.

- Use practice tracks.

There are practice tracks supplied with this book, but many more are available online. Make use of these, and don't forget to support the people who make them!

- Be patient.

You may feel as though you're not making any progress at first, but stick with it and have faith. With daily practice, you'll soon start to notice improvement.

Lastly, I hope the information I've shared in this book will prove helpful. This music has been a source of great joy in my life. I sincerely hope it will be the same for you. Now, go find your inner Gypsy!

Recommended Listening

Recording	Label
Django Reinhardt, *The Classical Early Recordings in Chronological Order*	JSP Records
Django Reinhardt, *The Best of Django Reinhardt*	Blue Note
Birelli Lagrene, *Gypsy Project & Friends*	Dreyfus
Angelo Debarre and Ludovic Beir, *Entre Amis*	Le Chant Du Monde
The Rosenberg Trio, *Seresta*	Polydor, Verve
Dorado Schmitt, *Live at the Kennedy Center*	SP Productions
Tchavolo Scmitt, *Seven Gypsy Nights*	Le Chant Du Monde
Fapy Lafertin & Le Jazz, *Swing Guitars*	Lejazzetal
Jimmy Rosenberg, *Django's Tiger (Swinging with Hot Club de Norvège)*	Hot Club Records
Yorgui Loeffler, *For Magnio*	Night & Day
The Hot Club of San Francisco, *Claire De Lune*	Hot Club Records
Les Doigts de l'Homme, *1910*	Cristal Records, Lamastrock
Adrien Moignard and Gonzalo Bergara, *Clasico*	CD Baby
Samy Daussat, *La petite famille*	Amazon Music
Romane, *Djangovision*	Frémeaux & Associés
Joscho Stephan, *Django Forever*	Acoustic Music Records

ABOUT THE AUTHORS

Jeff Magidson

Jeff Magidson has been a professional musician and educator for over 30 years. Born in San Francisco, he learned the rudiments at an early age from his parents who both were musicians. He became proficient at a number of instruments but decided to make guitar his main focus. In 1983, his studies took him to France. It was there that he first heard the music of Django Reinhardt. "I was mostly playing blues at the time, but if you are a guitar player, all roads eventually lead to Django, especially the French roads." After his studies, Jeff stayed in France another 20 years, touring the European continent with different bands. He returned to the states in 2004 and became the music director at Red House Studios, a San Francisco Bay Area music school. In 2005, he and his wife (an excellent rhythm guitarist and vocalist) both joined the renowned Hot Club of San Francisco led by Paul Mehling. After ten years, they decided to part ways with the band to focus more on their own Gypsy jazz project, Duo Gadjo. Gadjo is the Romani word for "outsider."

Dave Rubin

Dave Rubin is a New York City blues guitarist, teacher, author, and journalist. He has played with Son Seals, Honeyboy Edwards, Steady Rollin' Bob Margolin, Billy Boy Arnold, Johnny Copeland, Chuck Berry, James Brown's JBs, the Drifters, Marvelettes, Coasters, and the Campbell Brothers. In addition, he has performed on the *Blues Alley* TV show in Philadelphia and *New York Now* in the city and has made commercials for Mountain Dew and the Oreck company.

Dave has been an author for Hal Leonard for over 30 years, writing books in series such as *Inside the Blues*, *Signature Licks*, *Guitar School*, *Play Like*, and other assorted titles. He was the musical director for the Star Licks DVD series *Legends of the Blues*, as well as being featured in the *12-Bar Blues* accompanying video for his book that was nominated for a Paul Revere Award in 1999.

As a journalist, Dave has written for *Guitar Player*, *Guitar World*, *Guitar One*, *Living Blues*, *Guitar Shop*, and *Blues Access* magazines. Dave was the recipient of the 2005 Keeping the Blues Alive award in journalism from the Blues Foundation in Memphis, Tennessee.